Introduction

David Wilson

On Thursday 7 October 1971 sometime after nine o'clock Catherine Masterson climbed the stairs of her house in Avenham Lane in Preston, and went to bed. Later she was joined by her daughter Caroline who got into bed with her mother, perhaps for warmth and comfort, and eventually both fell asleep. A few hours later at about half past two in the morning they realised that someone else was in the bedroom, and that he had a knife. Catherine and Caroline were lucky. Despite the intruder carrying a weapon, their screams were loud and constant enough to scare him away. Both were badly shaken by this frightening episode, but Catherine's minor injuries from the intruder's attempts to stab her did not prevent her from being released from the Preston Royal Infirmary the following day.

When she got home she noticed that some of the clothes that she had hung out to dry in the backyard had been slashed and torn, and she drew the detective from the Lancashire Constabulary's attention to these thinking that they might be useful as evidence. She could not give much of a description of the intruder, except that he had been dressed only in his underpants and a T-shirt, but her daughter Caroline remembered that he 'looked about 30, was tall, medium build, with very black hair, which was curly'.

• • •

This is the story of Anthony Alexandrovich—known universally as 'Alex'—and his 29-year fight against his confession and conviction as a seventeen-year-old for the aggravated burglary of the Masterson's house, wounding with intent to do GBH to Catherine Masterson, and assault occasioning ABH against Caroline Masterson. Twenty-two of these years were spent in prison where Alex was a discretionary life sentenced prisoner, and where he steadfastly maintained his innocence. He continues to do so after release, and at the time of writing is taking his case through the Criminal Cases Review Commission (CCRC), which was set up in 1995 to investigate alleged miscarriages of justice.

It is no longer shocking to think that our criminal justice system—the 'best in the World'—produces miscarriages. We've got used to the fact that evidence can be fabricated, confessions forged, and that our police can be as corrupt as anyone else's can. And as the Birmingham Six beget the Guildford Four, who in turn beget the Bridgewater Four,

Stefan Kiszko, the Tottenham Three, and the countless others who by now rarely make it into our newspapers and our consciousness, the case of Alex appears just another story in the sea of stories about the failures of criminal justice. Yet it is much more than this, not just because Alex's story is so awful and compelling—he seems to have come straight out of a Kafka novel—but rather because justice has still not been done. There has been no happy ending; no apology for the lost years; no compensation for a life that has been spent in prisons the length and breadth of England; no end to the probation officers, and the threat of being returned to prison—a life licence, after all, lasts for *life;* and above all no sense of putting the past behind. That is where Alex lives—in the past, because it is there that the wrong was done, and so he cannot face the future until that wrong is made right. Released in July 1993, an extraordinary long time to have served for offences of the kind in question, and more than double the average length of time served by someone convicted of murder, Alex remains imprisoned. He is not imprisoned by prison officers and prison governors, or even politicians. He is imprisoned by injustice, and this book is an attempt to make right that injustice.

The first half of the book is made up of Alex's own attempt to put his story down on paper. It is called *Prison Chronicles* and deals with some aspects of Alex's case, and is largely set in the prisons he encountered during the early years of his sentence. As such the chronicles provide a fascinating glimpse of the origins and realities of the 'dispersal system' which had been set up after the 1966 Mountbatten Report, which had investigated prison security following the escapes of some of the Great Train Robbers, and the spy George Blake. Mountbatten had recommended that all potential escapers should be housed together in a special prison that was to be constructed on the Isle of Wight, and which was to be named Vectis. Ultimately this recommendation was not accepted, and instead a policy of dispersing the more difficult prisoners within six or seven prisons was adopted. These prisons became known as 'dispersals'.

Mountbatten had more luck with his recommendation that all prisoners should be given one of four security classifications. These classifications are A, B, C, and D. The lowest security classification is Category D, and this applies to prisoners who can reasonably be trusted in open conditions. Category A, the highest security category, is reserved for those prisoners whose escape would be highly dangerous to the public or the police or the security of the state, no matter how unlikely that escape might be, and for whom the aim must be to make escape impossible. Alex, barely 18, was one of the youngest Category A prisoners, and he describes the reality of living with this classification

The Longest Injustice

The Strange Story of Alex Alexandrowicz

Alex Alexandrowicz spent 22 years in some of Britain's most notorious gaols much of this time as a Category A high security prisoner. *The Longest Injustice* includes his own *Prison Chronicles* — a first hand account in which he explains why he believes he was wrongly convicted (a matter currently with the Criminal Cases Review Commission) and vividly recreates his experiences of the early years following his arrest. Institutionalised by the system and apprehensive of the outside world he now lives alone in Milton Keynes where he continues the long fight to clear his name from a flat which has grown to resemble a prison cell.

David Wilson is Professor of Criminal Justice and Course Director for the MA in Criminal Justice, Policy and Practice at the University of Central England in Birmingham. He is the former Head of Prison Officer and Operational Training for HM Prison Service, a post from which he resigned in 1997. At the time he was described by *The Observer* as the 'highest high flyer' in the Prison Service. He is a regular commentator on penal and criminal justice matters, including as co-presenter of the BBC 1 TV series *Crime Squad.* He also presented Channel 4's *Hard Cell* and is the editor of the *Howard Journal.* His previous books include *The Prison Governor: Theory and Practice* (1997) and *What Everyone in Britain Should Know About Crime and Punishment* (1998).

The Longest Injustice
The Strange Story of Alex Alexandrowicz

Published 1999 by
WATERSIDE PRESS
Domum Road
Winchester SO23 9NN
Telephone or Fax 01962 855567
INTERNET:watersidepress@compuserve.com

ISBN Paperback 1 872 870 45 7

Cataloguing-in-Publication Data A catalogue record for this book can be obtained from the British Library.

Printing and binding Antony Rowe Ltd, Chippenham

Cover design John Good Holbrook Ltd, Coventry using an original illustration by Peter Cameron.

Peter Cameron started painting whilst serving a ten and a half year prison sentence and came to terms with his imprisonment by making it the subject of his art. He is one of the 'Waterside 23' whose stories are told in *Going Straight After Crime and Punishment* compiled by Angela Devlin and Bob Turney, Waterside Press, 1999. Peter Cameron is now a freelance artist and can be contacted at The Hub, 9-13 Berry Street, Liverpool. Telephone 0151 709 0889.

The Longest Injustice

The Strange Story
of
Alex Alexandrowicz

Alex Alexandrowicz

David Wilson

WATERSIDE PRESS
WINCHESTER

*This book is dedicated to all those who didn't make it
and especially to all victims of British justice.*

The Longest Injustice

CONTENTS

WATERSIDE PRESS
WINCHESTER

---

[1] Alex's real name is *Anthony* Alexandrowicz, but he is known to everyone as *Alex* — an abbreviation of his surname.

Acknowledgements for Alex Alexandrowicz

John Ashton, Bill Jarvis, Bill McCoid, Joan Bronnimman, Alis Joyner, Maurice Chamberlain, Kevin Fegan, Melanie Fegan, Gillian Price, Robin Thornber, Andy Holt, Rose Pearce, Penny Fitzgerald, Steven Coogan, Kate Holdom, Radio Lancaster University, Irene Schimeld, Margaret Gateley, Richard Varley, Elspeth Varley, Andy Hood, Laurie and Jackie, Mike Spencer, Sue Oliver, Chris Kine, Janet Bowers, Alan Last, Andy Holt, Tessa O'Neil, Jeremy Corbin, Crowie, Dick Meadows, Fiona Fullerton, Edward Fitzgerald, Judi Kemish, Peter Beaumont, Nusse and Children, Geoff Hammond, Phil Hartwell, Steve Larner, Steve Lannigan, Sean Kinsella, Noel Gibson, Estella Ramos, Carlos Ramos, Paul Hill, Dave Rose, Andrew McKenzie, SO Gray, Dave Small, John Stead, John Beebe, Vivien Heilbron QC, Scott Dunsford, Dave King, Darren Foster, Lilian Temple, Phil Peratin and Debbie for putting up with me as she does.

Also, Dr Eric Cullen, my best friend.

Acknowledgements for David Wilson

Eric Cullen, Mike Sheldrick, Bryan Gibson, Stephen Shaw, Anne Maquire, Doug Sharp, and Barbara McCalla who typed the manuscript with her customary speed and efficiency.

in several of the new, tough dispersal prisons where he would mix with some of the most notorious offenders in the country. What was the danger that Alex posed to the public, the police, or the security of the state should he ever have attempted to escape? In attempting to answer these questions Alex's story begins to take on some fantastic, and bizarre twists and turns.

• • •

Perhaps the easiest place to start is with the danger that Alex might pose to members of the public. After all he had just been convicted of an aggravated burglary, during which a member of the public had been stabbed. Leaving aside the relatively minor nature of the injuries that the victim received, and the fact that Alex denies that he actually committed this offence, is there anything in his background that might suggest that he posed a danger to the public?

Alex was born on 8 February 1953, and first came to the attention of the authorities when he started to run away from home to escape his domineering and aggressive father. Aged about 12, he was committed to the care of the local authority and from then on he started to abscond from local authority homes. In June 1968, at Nelson Borough Juvenile Court, he was found guilty of stealing property from a market stall, to the value of £5.8s.10d, and was committed to approved school. So starts Alex's criminal career. He was to appear in the juvenile court on two further occasions in 1968, and then in 1969 he was sent to borstal on two counts of housebreaking. He served ten months in borstal, and was released on 17 August 1970. In October of that year he was sentenced to 18 months imprisonment for housebreaking, whereby he had posed as an electricity board employee but had then threatened the 15-year-old female occupant with a penknife which he had been using—until disturbed—to prise the doorlock. When she had become hysterical he ran away. His sentence for this offence ended on 24 September 1971, just 14 days before the burglary at the Masterson's house.

Does all this suggest that there is a pattern emerging of aggravated house burglary, committed by a troubled young man drifting from one sentence to another? At first glance the facts would seem to suggest that this is a reasonable conclusion to make, especially as Alex also seems to have asked for 37 other burglaries to be taken into consideration (usually called 'TICs'). Yet this is where Alex's story begins the first of it's many twists—twists that are at the very heart of this book.

Alex had been in care since he was 12, and thereafter in one institution after another. He could barely read or write, and was relatively immature and inarticulate. His background in homes and approved schools had made him compliant, malleable, deferential, and open to suggestion from those who exercised authority over him. In short Alex usually did as he was told. In particular he was used to accepting guilt, and asking for offences to be taken into consideration so that the police could clear them up, whether or not they were actually offences committed by him—a relatively common phenomenon. What is more, unbeknown to Alex when he had committed the two offences of housebreaking (under the pre-Theft Act 1998 law) for which he had received his borstal training, the houses that he had broken into had belonged to two senior police officers, one an assistant chief constable, and the other an inspector. Alex says that had been warned that if he ever came near the Preston area again his feet 'would not touch the ground'. Unfortunately for Alex he did go back, and he was arrested for the Masterson burglary having broken into an office building where he had been sleeping rough. His run of bad luck did not end there. One of the investigating officers was the inspector whose house Alex had broken into in October 1970.

• • •

Alex confessed to the Masterson break in, but this confession has to be put in context. After his arrest, Alex was questioned in circumstances that would now be disallowed, and even at the time were suspect. For example, he was kept awake for 48 hours, given inadequate food, and denied access to a lawyer. The police worded the confession—parts of which are at odds with the statements made by the Mastersons—and Alex signed it accordingly having been assured that he would receive only a short sentence. Not only that, the police had an ace up their collective sleeve. Nelson in Lancashire was known as 'Little Moscow', due to the large number of Russian émigrés who lived there, and some time previously Alex had visited the Russian Embassy in London in an effort to trace his Ukrainian grandparents. During the interview about the Masterson burglary, two plain clothes policemen whom Alex was told had come to see him from Liverpool, entered the interview room, and asked Alex about his visit to London. They also showed him a photograph of Alex sitting outside the Russian Embassy with a 'counsellor' whom Alex knew as Igor Laptev. Four days before Alex was arrested, Igor Laptev, in reality First Secretary at the Russian Embassy had been expelled along with 104 other Russians on spying charges. Alex says he was advised that if he did not own up to the Masterson burglary, then his father might end up deported also, and that it would be better for all concerned if Alex went inside for a couple of years 'until things quietened down'.

So Alex pleaded guilty. As a consequence no witnesses were called to the trial who might have pointed out that far from looking like the description provided by Caroline Masterson—'about 30, tall, medium build, with very black hair, which was curly'—Alex was of a different build, some 13 years younger, and had brown hair. Nor did Alex complain that it was the police who had written his statement, or that, as he alleges, it was they who had entered incriminating evidence into a notebook which he had kept and who made him handle a sheath knife, which wasn't his, but which was later presented at court as the knife with which he had stabbed Catherine Masterson. Alex's first contact with a solicitor was just before his appearance at court, and even his parents were not advised about what was happening. So Alex appears before Mr Justice Cantley very much alone, and who in the face of the information presented to him, and in the absence of *any* mitigation, or indeed opposition to what was being said accepts Alex's guilty plea, and sentences him to life.

By any standards a life sentence for an aggravated burglary is unusual, and disproportionate to the harm Alex was accused of causing. Did he really pose that much danger to the public or the police? Or instead was the sentence a reflection of the danger that he might pose to the state? In any event this is only the first half of the story.

● ● ●

The second half of the story concerns the extraordinary length of time that Alex spent in prison—as already indicated, double the average length of time served by someone convicted of murder—and his fight to be released. Indeed that he was released at all was as a consequence of the impact of European legislation on our penal system, and how discretionary life sentenced prisoners were dealt with, rather than a change of heart about Alex by the Home Office. And, as more people became aware of Alex's case, and ultimately he had a play and TV documentary written about him, which led to the foundation of a support group, new and bizarre evidence would emerge as to why he was being kept in prison. Bill Jarvis, for example, a Birmingham magistrate whom I interviewed at length for the Channel 4 series *Clear My Name*, and who took up Alex's case remembers going to the Home Office, and being mistakenly shown Alex's file. Bill explains that in the file he remembers seeing a photograph of Alex, taken out of doors, in the company of someone fitting Igor Laptev's description with the words 'This man should not be released for 30 years' hand-written on the corner. Did they believe that Alex was some sort of 'sleeper', about to become activated by his Russian spymaster? Indeed, it should be remembered that the Mountbatten Enquiry was initiated as a result of the escape of the spy George Blake from HMP Wormwood Scrubs in 1965, and that Alex's arrest comes only six years later.

● ● ●

The second half of this book attempts to bring *Prison Chronicles* up to date by sketching in what happens to Alex after he finishes his story in 1981. This is important, for readers of *Prison Chronicles* might get the impression that Alex's time inside was spent getting into greater or lesser amounts of trouble with the prison authorities. This was not the case, especially in the second half of Alex's sentence. I have written this part of the book, and in tribute to Alex's title have called that part *After the Chronicles End*. Indeed Alex was to spend another 12 years in prison after his *Prison Chronicles* end. The most significant portion of the remainder of his sentence was spent at HMP Grendon, the only prison in Britain to operate as a therapeutic community, and where Alex came into contact with one of the unsung heroes of his case—the prison's former principal psychologist Eric Cullen. I also worked at the prison as a Governor during Alex's time there, and came to know him and Eric well. In fact, as will be described, it was me who met Alex at the gates of HMP Grendon after he had absconded from HMP Leyhill to draw attention to his case. As research for this book I interviewed Eric Cullen about his memories of and observations about Alex, and was given access to the voluminous files which he has kept almost since their first contact. These include not only internal Prison Service reports, but also correspondence about Alex between Eric and various politicians working at the Home Office at that time, including David Mellor and Angela Rumbold; newspaper accounts of Alex's case in *The Guardian*; poems and pieces of journalism written by Alex; the text of a TV documentary about Alex made by Granada Television—*The Curious Case of Alex*; and the text of a play inspired by the case by Kevin Fegan, called *Rule 43*.

I also have access to the original documents used at Alex's trial. Where I can I draw on this documentary evidence, and quote directly from pieces that are within the public domain in the hope that this will give Alex a voice. Clearly I cannot quote directly without permission from internal Prison Service documents, and I have avoided doing so except where these have been referred to previously within Alex's journalism, or in *The Curious Case of Alex*. Nonetheless these documents have informed my understanding of what happened to Alex, and have thus been woven into the background and context of what I describe. I have also met with Alex on a number of occasions since his release from prison. First as preparation for an attempt to film his case for the Channel 4 series *Clear My Name,* and thereafter in an attempt to get down on paper the remainder of his story. Ultimately, for reasons that he has been unable to articulate to me, Alex felt unable to continue to co-operate with this project beyond the meetings which had taken place, but he is fully aware that this book is being written in the extended form that is (the publishers originally acquired the rights to *Prison Chronicles* but soon became aware that there was more to the story and that Alex himself was unable to piece the remainder together), and that Eric and others are contributing to the book.

Alex's knowledge that the book is being written in this form does not absolve me from thinking carefully about some of the ethical questions that inevitably surround completing a book of this kind. After all, the reality that is being described is Alex's, and the first part of the book is his own work. I did not edit or contribute to that part of the book, although I have discussed it at some length with him, and have read it thoroughly several times. It would obviously have been preferable if Alex had finished the book himself, but for various reasons he did not seem able to complete the manuscript. Not only that—he subsequently felt unable to continue with the interview schedule which we had agreed to, which would have allowed me to sketch in the remainder of *Prison Chronicles* directly informed by his own memories and recollections. Indeed as a consequence there was a stage in the writing of the book when I feared that, practically it could not be completed. That I was able to do so (and also I hope continue to give Alex a voice albeit filtered through me, printed materials and documents, and through interviews with others) was only one half of the ethical question which I believed had to be resolved. The second part of this question is more philosophical and abstract, but nonetheless is just as important as the practicalities of completing the writing.

The second part of this ethical question has many layers. At a more general level I had to be certain that Alex actually wanted the book to be completed; that he wanted some 'closure' to this awful reality of his past. In trying to find an answer to this question smaller but equally important questions continued to emerge. Did Alex withdraw from the project because he no longer felt 'in control' of how the story was being written and completed? Was there a problem in that I am a former prison governor—part of 'the system' that used to control his life and destiny? Ultimately in deciding to continue with the book I felt comfortable that these questions had been positively answered, and I constantly attempted to check these answers out with Alex, Alex's supporters and friends. In particular it should also be remembered that it was Alex who had approached a publisher with his story, and wrote numerous articles about his circumstances in the press. Clearly he was not shy about publicity, and indeed we initially renewed our own acquaintance through the lens of a TV camera. Similarly Alex is continuing to fight his conviction through the CCRC—a clear signal that he wants the closure that a book of this kind might in the right circumstances bring. Finally I was also re-assured that Alex had 'nothing against me personally', and encouraged me to do as I wished in a letter he wrote to Bryan Gibson, co-proprietor of Waterside Press. As a consequence I have continued with the book, and although these ethical questions still nag at me I hope that I do justice to Alex's story.

Happily, having sent Alex a draft copy of the completed manuscript he once again felt able to participate in the project. This participation has allowed me to further inform *After the Chronicles End* and I have been able to re-work the last section about what has happened to Alex since his release. Alex was also able to 'acknowledge' those acquaintances and friends who were of assistance and support to him, and even made suggestions as to the cover of the book. He did not ask for any changes to the text which I had written, which gives me some confidence that in thinking through the ethical questions after his initial withdrawal was worth the trouble and effort.

• • •

Neither Alex nor myself have attempted to produce a 'scholarly book'. *Prison Chronicles* is a powerful autobiography of painful memories and reflections. *After the Chronicles End* attempts to bring that story up to date, and also provide a context for what has been described. We have rarely used footnotes, and do not provide a series of references. However in the passages which I have written, and where it does not interfere with the text, I have attempted to draw the reader's attention to the sources that I have used, and how these can be followed up for those who are interested. As will be appreciated some of these sources are interviews conducted by myself in the course of researching the book, and in turn these are infused by my own memories of Alex, and my personal experiences of working as a prison governor for 14 years. Again, for those who are interested I have attached to the book a short *Guide to Further Reading*, including more scholarly works which deal with life sentenced prisoners, and HM Prison Service.

The final sections of the book attempt to describe what has happened to Alex after his release from prison. Unlike Hollywood films which see the release from prison as then being the 'happy ever after', the experience of ex-offenders is far from the stuff of the movies. Anyone who has spent a significant amount of time inside is fundamentally damaged by that experience. At the most obvious level relationships have suffered, and families have often been broken up. It is difficult to get work, or even accommodation, and there is the constant problem of having to find money. The temptation to commit more crime is constant, despite the ever-present Probation Service. All of these difficulties are great enough for any offender, but they are doubly so for ex-offenders like Alex who have to survive on a life licence.

Since his release, Alex has been living in Milton Keynes where he can be close to the small circle of friends that support him. He has not found work, and is constantly worried and anxious about the future. His health is poor, and Eric Cullen has been worried on more than one occasion that Alex might be close to the end. Nonetheless he has survived, and on one or two occasions I have even seen him fired with enthusiasm, although these enthusiasms are often related to his determination to take his case through the CCRC, and have the wrongs of the past put right. To his eternal credit, and perhaps revealing something of the person that Alex is, he has not committed any further crimes since his release from prison almost six years ago. At the time of writing this introduction Alex is 46-years-old, and he has spent almost 30 years of his life in institutions of one kind or another. Unsurprisingly in many ways he is totally institutionalised. One manifestation of this is his belief that—ultimately—the truth will win out, no matter what the odds. Let us hope that his is not a naïve belief and that at long last the longest injustice might come to an end.

PRISON CHRONICLES

Prisoner 789959
Alex Alexandrowicz[1]

---

[1] Alex's real name is *Anthony* Alexandrowicz, but he is known to everyone as *Alex*. As he explains in *Prison Chronicles*, many people found his surname difficult to pronounce — and began shortening it to 'Alex' (see p. 31)

CHAPTER ONE

Travelling back from Manchester Crown Court, was very different from the journey to it. On the way there, I had been handcuffed to another prisoner, on a bus half full of men being taken to court. But on the way back, I was handcuffed to a screw and the transport was a taxi. There were three screws altogether. Two in the back and one in the front next to the driver.

The reason for the security was clear. I had just been sentenced to two life sentences, for crimes I had not had anything to do with—GBH[2] and aggravated burglary.

It is difficult trying to think back all those years to what was going through my mind as the taxi sped out of Manchester towards Risley Remand Centre in Cheshire. They were not ordered thoughts. I had been given a liberal dose of a strong tranquilliser before setting out that morning, the effect of which was still with me. Somewhere, was the voice of the judge saying 'Life imprisonment on both counts ...'

• • •

I was 18 years old and it was three days before Christmas 1971. I do remember the screws saying, that a life sentence was one that could mean months, that the Home Secretary could release me at any time. Nothing at all was said about the average term for a lifer being eleven years ...! All the way back to Risley the screws kept emphasising that a life sentence was not a very long sentence.

No logic to that. I did realise that the screws were making attempts to keep me quiet, to prevent me shouting and wrestling with them in the car. I knew that. I shut out the sound of their voices altogether for a while.

The outside world was one eighth of an inch away. It sped by. Every so often the car stopped at a traffic light and I could have reached out and touched people walking by on the pavement outside, if the window had been wound down ... shops were lit-up with coloured lights in their windows, the tinsel hanging in loops, the smiles of the shopkeepers warmer than usual. Children were not walking with their mothers, they were skipping along as excited as anything, held in the fantasy of Christmas and adding to it.

I was praying that the taxi would crash and that I would be killed. I knew how far away Risley was and I felt each mile slip by as though

---

[2] Causing grievous bodily harm

it was a physical blow and the nearer we came to the prison the more edgy the screws became. They could feel my vibes. Then, there it was, the high wall with the razor-wire looped around the top . . . the great wooden doors sliding open and my heart racing in time with the car engine—and the gloom of the gatehouse as the doors closed behind, shutting out the daylight. The screws breathed with relief . . . I realised then that this was *their* world, *their* domain. In this world they were lords and kings, the prisoners were the subjects, the vassals.

The realisation washed over me as a dread tide, until I was submerged by it. I was taken out of the taxi and escorted into the reception block. I was given prison clothing and a number,

789959.

Normally, a new inmate would be seen in reception by a prison doctor, but I was told I was to be located in the hospital anyway, so there was no point.

•   •   •

The hospital block was a fairly modern structure. There were flower beds outside it. It looked nice, until you got inside. I was to discover that the prison administrators had a policy of camouflaging their buildings so that they were as pleasant to the eye as possible. Of course, within those buildings there was very little that could be so described. It was the first con I learned about.

Inside the hospital I was told I was to go into the ward, not into a single cell. They wanted to keep an eye on me—I realised that. All lifers are treated this way because the authorities expect a suicide bid.

A hospital screw led me up a flight of stairs towards the ward. A couple of cons squeezed past on their way down. They gave me a strange look and must have known where I was at. Inside the ward, there were perhaps ten or 12 beds, some of them made-up, others untidy. A few men were sitting around a TV set. I put my kit down on one of the beds and sat down on it. A hospital screw brought me a tot of medicine and told me to drink it. It was the same stuff I'd been given over the past two or three weeks. It made me sleepy. So I fell asleep.

When the teas were being served, I was woken up. I don't recall eating anything. But I had a few hours of consciousness where I had the opportunity to replay the day's events through my mind. Every minute of it seemed to come back, and become jumbled, and then clear again. Sentenced to *two* life sentences . . . What had happened? This was *my* life, not theirs. *Woof*—as far as I could figure it out I'd been set-up.

What a fool! *I hadn't committed those crimes! I was innocent!!!* There was a curious sensation of abstraction as if it was somebody else—that this wasn't happening to me. How *could* it be happening to me? The drugs bit into me and I was gone again.

• • •

Christmas Day was perceived through a haze. Inane Christmas songs came cheerfully from the TV set: *Ernie's Fastest Milkcart, Rudolph's Red Nose*. A young lad a couple of beds away had been screaming all night in his sleep, another had been crying, and yet another was a suicide attempt. They were sitting in front of the TV, mesmerised. No smiles. No laughter. One youth had thought that I was a murderer, and he asked for a change of bed, to one at the other end of the ward. He was wrong. But I could understand his view. Me with a double life sentence . . .

The windows had bars on them. Beyond was a small concrete and grass exercise area, coils of razor-wire adding an element of surrealism to the scene . . . projecting a chill to the already cold day. Anyone foolish enough to try to escape would be cut to ribbons, courtesy of the taxpayer. I would look through the windows, staring at that grey and harmful scene for long minutes at a time, turning away with a depression upon me. Sleep was a life-saver. The longer the sleep, the less of a day to deal with. Minutes were hours. Hours were days. A month was an eternity.

After Christmas I was called-up to be interviewed by the psychiatrist.

'Good Morning! Please sit down. I see that you have been sentenced to Life imprisonment . . . how do you feel about that . . . ?'

'The police told me to hold my hand up to the GBH and the aggravated burglary. They said I would be sent down for a couple of years if I pleaded guilty. That my father would be deported if I didn't play the game, or if I messed them about. I wasn't sentenced to two years was I?'

'Are you saying that you are innocent?'
'Yes'.
'I see'.

And so on. Nobody could then believe that the police would stitch someone up. Or perhaps they did believe it, but were not prepared to admit it. This was England. Such concepts were, if not unthinkable, at lease unutterable. The screws and the governors, the doctors and the probation officers were all able to justify their work, as long as they believed that they were banging villains up every night. If they thought otherwise they wouldn't be able to function.

The doctor called me up a couple of times to prescribe more dope. The psychiatrist made me play games with ink-blots. The chaplain wanted me to attend Sunday Service. The screws wanted me to do exactly as I was told. After a month of it I didn't know how I would survive another day. Every time I woke in the mornings, another day had arrived. Every day had to be taken separately. They each had a tomorrow, when the truth of my innocence would be established. Something would happen. The true culprit would be caught or would give himself up . . . But as each day went by, as each tomorrow came and went, no such thing happened. Live for today, then.

• • •

Two years earlier, I was on the run from an approved school. I was 16 years old. I had been in children's homes and then approved schools since I was 12. I kept running away. In the beginning, I would steal from shop counters when I was on the run. But as time went by I began breaking into houses. I always made sure the houses were empty and I always broke in during the daytime. I was a housebreaker.

I would take food from kitchens, and sometimes money, if it was lying about in view. I never ransacked rooms, though I wasn't doing it for kicks—but through need. I broke into a house in Houghton, near Preston in Lancashire. I didn't know who owned it but it turned out to be the assistant chief constable's house. At around the same time I broke into a house in Fulwood, Preston. I did not know that the house belonged to a police inspector . . .

When I was eventually caught the police inspector appeared in person at the juvenile court, sitting at Fulwood. He said I'd taken things which I hadn't. I told the magistrates that he was lying. After I had been put back in the police cells, the inspector came in and said he couldn't do anything now, but if ever I set foot in Preston again, he would see to it that 'my feet wouldn't touch the ground'. I was sent back to my approved school.

• • •

One year earlier I had gone to the Soviet Embassy in London in an effort to find out the whereabouts of my grandparents (on my father's side). I was referred to an official who said he was a counsellor. We went

outside and sat on a bench. It was the lunch hour. He had some
sandwiches in a paper bag. I told him what I wanted and he said he
would see what he could do. He did ask me some questions about my
father and whether I was born in this country. Did I go to a state
school? What did I want to be when I left school? He seemed curious but
not unpleasantly so. He gave me his name, Igor Laptev, and a 'phone
number. I was to ring the number after a few weeks and ask for him by
name; by which time, hopefully, he would have some news. I did not go
back to the Embassy, nor did I telephone the man. I had lost the 'phone
number anyway.

● ● ●

Early in the New Year, 1972, I was called-up by the PO[3] and told that I
was to be moved to Walton Gaol, Liverpool, where I was to begin
serving my sentence. At first I welcomed the news because it meant I
would be moved from Risley and that hospital ward full of screaming
vibes. I had begun to learn that pain and violence did not necessarily
have to be inflicted by physical blows. More than that, that in a
confined space shared with suffering people I was somehow able to feel
their pain and their torment . . . it was a new experience for me.
Perhaps, at Liverpool prison I would be given my own cell. Also, it
meant that I would be able to catch a glimpse of the outside world once
more.

Again I was moved in a taxi and escorted by three screws. It didn't
take long to reach Liverpool and the district of Walton. One of the
screws pointed out of the car window to a massive Victorian building,
where long tiers of cell windows could be seen. A high wall surrounded
the place, and on the road outside pedestrians were walking with their
heads down, as if to ignore the prison, to pretend it wasn't there.

The gates of the prison loomed up, on the right-hand side of the
road and as we approached they opened slowly, until the dark interior
of the gatehouse was exposed, inviting me into its depths. Try as I
might, over the next few years, I could not erase the memory of the
prison gates from the nightmares I was to have . . . The prison
gatehouse was the first shock, the realisation that one was entering,
literally, another world. Not a better world, but the opposite. The
gates would clang shut behind, like a Venus fly-trap enclosing its prey.
Such was the sensation.

I was escorted into the reception block, where the Risley screws
asked the Walton screws for my receipt, for my body. This was handed

---

[3] Principal officer

over and I was put into a tiny cubicle, a 'holding box', and the door to it was shut and locked. I had only sufficient space to stand or sit down. The box was three feet wide by four feet deep. I had never suffered from claustrophobia, but I tried to imagine those who did being locked into that tiny space. It would have been torture. I also thought that I wouldn't be kept in there for very long, but it was to be close to four hours before the doors opened again. I had cramp!

I was led to a long counter where three screws sat, maybe ten feet apart. The first screw had a sheet of paper in front of him and was making notes on it with a pen. As I approached, he looked up and gestured with a pen, to have me stand in front of him. He told me to strip off. As I did, each item of clothing was taken off me and catalogued on the sheet. One of the cons, a reception orderly, handed me a rough blue dressing-gown. The screw asked if I had any valuables; a watch, ring or chain? I said 'No'.

The second screw in line asked my religion, my next if kin. The third screw asked if I had any diseases or illnesses. I was told to stand on a set of scales to be weighed. Then measured. Finally, I was given a set of prison clothing and a bed-pack. Before putting on the clothes I was sent for a bath. The bath had six inches of water in it and the water was very hot. Because I was not allowed to add to the volume of water, I couldn't run the cold tap, so I swished the water about, to make a noise and went without the bath.

It was early evening before I as taken to the wing where I was to be located while at Walton. It was the YP[4] Wing. I was surprised that, although there were a number of other cons who had arrived during the day, also carrying bed-packs, I was the only one who was being individually escorted by a screw . . . the others were allowed to walk across to the wing in a group. I supposed it was because of the sentence I'd been given.

The wings at Walton were very different from the wings at Risley. The Walton wings were great cavernous halls, with rows of cells on four levels. To reach each level, it is necessary to climb narrow flights of iron stairs, just wide enough for one person to negotiate. Each row of cells was called a 'landing'; the 'Ones', Twos', 'Threes' and 'Fours'. I was taken to a cell on the Twos.

I had been handed a 'cell-card' before leaving reception. These recorded a prisoner's religion, diet, work classification (i.e. a person who is fit and able is classified One. An unfit person, perhaps an aged person, is classified Three), length of sentence and prison number. The card was displayed outside the inmate's cell door. In this way, I was

---

[4] Young prisoner

stripped of my citizen status and relegated to a number, who was fit and able, ate ordinary food and subscribed to the C of E religion. This information was displayed as it was so that a screw on the landing could tell at a glance what he wanted to know about a prisoner, without having to unlock the door and speak to him directly.

The screw who was escorting me led me onto the Two's. We went down the narrow landing and stopped at a cell door. The screw unlocked it and asked for my cell card which he slotted into the card holder on the back of the door. I also noticed another card there which was blank save for a large red capital 'A'. Again, I didn't give it much of a second thought.

The cell was not overly clean. It was relatively spacious, its walls rough brick with patches of paint peeling away from it. The last occupant had left his pin-ups on one of the walls, a frieze of naked women in different postures. There was a bucket in a corner which was the toilet, and which needed emptying—another gift from the last occupant—and which stank. I put down the bed-roll I'd been carrying, and sat down on the cot. The only other items of furniture were a small table and a school chair. Graffiti covered the back of the cell door, the wall next to the cot, even the mattress on the cot was liberally signed by past prisoners. I realised that there was no water-jug or wash-basin and immediately felt thirsty and dirty. I also realised that I was hungry; my last meal having been a small bowl of porridge, before leaving Risley that morning . . . God, that seemed like *days* ago . . . !

I hand-rolled a cigarette from a few dog-ends. I hadn't any more tobacco. As it burned down to the last eighth of an inch, that had gone too. I went for a piss. The bucket had a couple of inches of urine in the bottom, and a turd which was melting into liquid, stuck to the bottom of the bucket. I directed a stream of urine onto the turd and then threw up. To stop the vomit from falling onto the cot or onto the floor I had to put my face over the bucket.

Unrolling my bed-pack I found two sheets, a pillowcase, two blankets with other peoples' odours impregnating them, a water-jug (empty of course), a shaving brush and soap, a toothbrush and a bar of White Windsor soap. At ten o'clock I heard the night screw coming round switching the cell lights off. When he got to my cell however, he turned out the main light, but left the red night light on. Immediately I jumped up and knocked on the door. The night screw came back and I asked him to turn the red light off. He said that I was an 'A-Man' and the regulations said, that the red light had to be left on. I was about to argue, but thought better of it. The next morning I would find out what an A-Man was.

Sleep came with great difficulty. I was tired enough but other cons were shouting to each other, via the cell windows, yelling at each other, using the foulest language and threatening one another. Other cons were kicking their cell doors, the loud bangs reverberating through the wing, the hollow space of the hall acting as an echo-chamber. It was a madhouse.

● ● ●

I must have fallen into a waking sleep, a night spent in profound discomfort, the events of the day themselves a chronicle of a year's worth of the worst experiences.

CHAPTER TWO

The next morning I was awoken by a screw banging on the door. I heard him banging on all the doors, one after the other, for about the next 15 minutes; I thought the cell doors were about to be opened, but they weren't. It took another hour, before the screws started to 'unlock'.

• • •

The first thing that had to be done, was to slop-out the toilet buckets, then when that was done, we were allowed a further five minutes, to go and fetch hot water for a wash. I took the toilet bucket along with me to the recess, and stood in line, while other men poured their piss and shit into the sluice. The sluice, as usual, was clogged up, and the sewage simply floated around in a stagnant, evil-smelling mess. I was ashamed to empty my bucket, because it smelled so bad. But it had to be done. Surprisingly, nobody complained . . . ! I went to the landing screw and asked for a washbowl and towel. He asked me which cell I was in. When I told him, he became agitated, and ordered me back to my cell. He followed close behind and virtually shoved me inside, and banged the door shut. A bit later, the door was opened again, and a screw told me to go and get my breakfast. All the other cons had been banged-up again. There were only two others going for their breakfast with me, one of them wore yellow patches on the back of his jacket, and yellow stripes down his jeans . . . I wondered what that meant? I also noticed that we were being watched closely, by the screw who'd unlocked us, and by another one, on the ground-floor level, where the hotplate was.

'You just got here, then?', the con with the yellow patches asked.

He'd spoken as we were collecting our porridge. The stuff was being dished out by cons, wearing white jackets. These were the landing cleaners; part of their duties was to dish out the food at the hotplate. In addition to the porridge there was a tiny piece of bacon laid on. The con serving it gave me three pieces although I knew that I was only entitled to one.

'I got here yesterday', I said. 'Transferred from Risley'.
'We'll get a chance for a talk and a bit of exercise later on. How long are you doing?'
'Life'.

'Me too. If there's anything you need, let me know an' I'll tell you what to do. My name's Will. If you don't give 'em any trouble', he indicated the nearest screw, 'they won't give you any'.

I didn't answer. The three of us carried our metal food trays up the narrow staircase—I stumbled on one of the steps, but didn't fall. Those stairs took some getting used to. I found out that they were constructed in that way so that if there was a riot on one of the landings, the only way to reach the ground floor would be in single file . . . making it easier for the cons to be whacked over the head and captured. It made sense.

Again we were banged-up. At 9.30 am a screw opened the flap covering the Judas-hole, thumped on the door and asked if I wanted exercise. Of course I did. Yes. The exercise area was a small patch of ground outside one of the wings. I was with Will and the other con. Two screws and an alsation dog were positioned off to one side.

'What's your name then?', Will asked.
'Alex'.

Will nodded. The other lad was rolling a cigarette. He passed his tobacco tin on to Will and myself. He introduced himself as Phil. He'd also been 'lifed-off'. Both Will and Phil were murderers. Will was 19 and he'd served eight months. He came from Wigan. He explained why we were being singled out for the extra security.

'We're on the 'A' List. That is, you an' Phil are. I'm on both the 'A' List *and* the 'E' List . . . !'

Apparently, prisoners classified as 'A', were the ones, of all the prisoners in Britain, who must not be given the chance to escape. Will said he'd been told that there were only 20 or so such prisoners. All were classed as 'Threats to Society'.

'You're joking!'. I didn't believe that!
'He ain't joking mate', Phil said, blowing smoke from his nostrils. 'He's gone one better . . . he's Cat. A and a Cat. E'. He saw my lack of comprehension. 'A Cat. E is someone who's either escaped or tried to escape . . . the yellow patches are to make him visible, man'.

Woof. What was going down? Me, a threat to society? I couldn't believe it!

'Don't look so worried, man. It ain't so bad. You'll see. Have you got any baccy?'

'Do we get paid here, or what?'

Will said 'We get three shillings every Thursday morning. You got your tin with you?'
    I had yet to acquire a tobacco tin, but I had some paper in my jacket pocket. Both cons put some tobacco in it, together with Rizlas and matches. 'We help each other here, you see', Will explained.

'How come we got extra food at breakfast?', I asked.
'That's what I mean', Phil said. 'Bein' on the 'A' List. We get looked after'. I wondered what the day was going to bring. Did we go to work? Did we get any association time later on? What time was dinner? What about letters . . . were we allowed to have a free letter? And what about visits?
'Have you got anyone to come and see you man?', Will asked.
'My Mom will visit, and my Dad, I guess. Once they get told what the procedure is'.

Phil said I'd be given a 'reception letter' and a VO[1] later in the day. If I didn't get it I'd have to remind one of the screws. I noticed another screw come over to the exercise area, and shout my name. Will said I was probably being called-up for the first of the interviews I'd be getting. It would probably be either a governor's or probation call-up.

'See you later, Alex'.

• • •

The escort screw said I was being called-up by the assistant governor. As I was being shepherded through the wings, I was conscious of other cons clocking me. We crossed over a ground floor landing, which was being scrubbed by a team of YPs. I felt guilty walking over their newly-scrubbed landing, but the screw seemed to take a delight in it; he could have taken me round the cleaned part, it would have meant a couple of seconds delay, no more. We arrived at the chief officer's office. The screw knocked quietly on the door, opened it and announced:

'Alexandrowicz, Sir'.

He didn't pronounce it properly. Mind you, not many people did. I was shown into a carpeted room. The carpet felt very strange underfoot.

---

[1] Visiting order

Sitting at a desk was a man in civvies, who looked cheerful enough. A brief flicker of a smile, before he got down to business.

'So', he said, glancing from me to the file on the desk in front of him, 'Alexandrowicz is it? What's that? Russian? Polish?'
'Dad's Ukrainian, governor'.

I'd already made up my mind never to address any of these people as 'Sir'. He spotted it straight away, of course. He didn't pursue it.

'Hmm. I see you are serving a life sentence. I try to see all the lifers who get sent here. Well. I think you will find that your time in prison can be spent quite constructively. There are various programmes . . . are you interested in education? No? Bible classes perhaps? We have a first-rate chaplain. The important thing is to stay clear of trouble; if you have any problems, you can ask to see one of us and we'll be more than willing to help. During the rest of this week, you won't be required to work. Most of your time will be taken up in various interviews, so that we get to know you . . .'

'Governor, why have I been put on Category A?'
'Well obviously the police aren't too happy with you. You are serving a life sentence. Two life sentences. Presumably the people you killed have something to do with it'.
'I haven't killed anyone governor, I was convicted of GBH and aggravated burglary'.
'I see . . .'
'But the best of it is I can't work out why . . . I reckon I must have been fitted-up'.

I knew I shouldn't have said that. He thought for a while, then became terse and said that would be all. The screw was waiting outside the door to escort me elsewhere. I could see through the doors, I could see the assistant governor writing in my file 'Trouble-maker'.

• • •

There was no more exercise later on, after all, because the rest of the day was taken up with interviews. I was able to visit the clothing store, and get some clothes that actually fitted. Then down to the library to pick up a few books. Over to the hospital, to see the doctor—I had been on drugs at Risley and the doctor wanted to renew them. He asked how I was feeling, and I couldn't answer, because I couldn't find the right words. It was a pretty stupid question anyway.

And everywhere I went I was accompanied by a screw. If I went to the toilet, he was there waiting for me to come out. There was a small red book he carried, which was a record of everything I did; the book was a log. All the minutes of my day were accounted for, from the moment I was unlocked in the morning, to the time I was banged up in the evening. My photograph was fixed inside the book, like a passport. One thing I did take up with the doctor, was the red light that'd been left on all night in my cell. I explained that it stopped me from sleeping, but he said the only thing he could do was prescribe a sleeper. I think he put me on Mogadon.

• • •

I was clocked by a lot of prisoners as I was being led to and from all day. They knew I was Cat. A because of the book carried by the screw. I was left alone . . . which was just as well because I was a lousy fighter; violence was something I hated, it hurt people. The longest interview I had was with a woman who may have been a psychologist or something, I can't remember exactly. It lasted for more than an hour.

I entered the office in mid-afternoon. She introduced herself and asked me to sit down.

'What do people call you . . . ?'
'Alex. It's not my Christian name, but I've got used to it. It's because my surname is hard for people to pronounce, so they shorten it down to "Alex"'.
'That's fine. Now let's see . . . ' She briefly studied my file which was on the table in front of her. 'You were born in February eighth, 1953. That makes you what . . . ? Just turned 19, yes? You come from Nelson in Lancashire and your parents still live there . . . you have a sister who is four years younger than you. Hmm. You were arraigned before Lancaster Assizes last November, and sentenced to two life sentences, at Manchester Crown Court, on December third last year?'

'That's right'.
'You pleaded guilty to GBH and to aggravated burglary . . .?'
'Yes . . . '
'You've been placed on Category A. Do you know why?'
'I've no idea'.
'Tell me something about yourself, Alex. You were put into care when you were 12 . . . you've been in institutions ever since . . . Why were you put into care?'

I looked at her. She hadn't been writing anything down. She wasn't old, maybe middle twenties; she sat with her elbow on the table, and her chin in her hand, eyebrows raised. I wondered briefly what had decided her to work in a prison . . . she seemed a decent sort for a prison worker. My prison experience so far—my time at Risley—had been a black and lifeless one. Spiritless. Profoundly joyless. Most of the prison staff I'd met were grey, patronising people. I disliked them as only a captive can dislike his gaolers. Whatever their brief was, it wasn't to bring light into the shadows. Most of it was to learn personal details so that they could more easily control the individual.

'I ran away from home a couple of times'.
'Why?'
'Because my Dad was always beating me up. My Mom would always jump in to stop him, and he'd turn on her and beat her'.
'Why would he want to beat you up, Alex?'
'When I was a baby I was enuretic. You understand? I used to wet the bed. I know my Dad thought I was doing it on purpose. So as soon as I was old enough to stand being hit, I think I was about three or four years old, he started using a belt on me. I sure wasn't doing it on purpose! I went into hospital when I was nine or ten and even the doctors couldn't do anything. I was enuretic until last year . . .'
'How did you feel about it?'
'I felt ashamed. I still do. I was scared to go to sleep. It was worse when I was put into the children's home. I was put in a dormitory, you see. The other kids were on to me all the time. It was hell. It was hard facing each new day because I knew the reaction it would bring. I didn't understand why I was different from the other kids; I couldn't understand what was wrong with me. And so I begun to run away from the children's homes. They kept putting me in more secure places, to try to make it harder to do a bunk, but I always found a way, and I'd be gone. No one seemed to know why I was doing it; they just kept saying I was running away to be a nuisance. And the only answer they had was to keep putting me in more stricter places . . .'

'Go on . . .'
'To them I was a kid who was anti-authority, who just kept running away to cause trouble'.
'How long did you go missing for?'
'Days at a time'.
'But how did you survive? Didn't you get hungry? Where did you sleep?'

'Well, at first I'd go into shops and steal things from the counters. Bars of chocolate, biscuits. I'd sleep in peoples' coal sheds, or in the toilets on railway stations. But after they sent me to approved school, I found out about housebreaking. I'd wait until halfway through the morning, or afternoon, when I knew that most people were out. I'd find a house and go and knock on the door. If no one answered, I'd go round the back and do the same again. When I was sure there was no one in, I'd find an open window and go and raid the kitchen. If there was money left lying around, I'd take that too. Then I'd be gone. I never ransacked drawers or rooms or anything . . . '

'Did you understand how wrong it was?'
'To break into houses like that? I knew it was wrong . . . I always thought that if the people who owned the house knew it was a kid who was hungry, they wouldn't mind as much'.
'That was your excuse?'
'Yes'.
'A crap excuse, Alex . . . '
'Kids have a way of looking at things differently'. I rolled a smoke and lit it. 'I've been brought up in places where crazy values are taught. Sure it's a crap excuse. But try sleeping on a heap of coal and going without a meal for a week. Soon you don't mind much where your next bit of food's coming from, as long as it stops you from starving . . . and I'd have starved anyway rather than turn myself in!'
'You get angry easily'.
'With good reason. You wouldn't understand unless you've been through the same situations that I have. I haven't shared your life with you. I wouldn't understand much of your views, or opinions. We've been taught differently'.
'That's no excuse for doing wrong. You don't have to be taught right and wrong. It's something you learn instinctively. But if it's any consolation to you, I do understand . . . you aren't the first prisoner I've interviewed. Tell me some more. Help me to understand better . . . When were you sent to approved school . . . ?'
'It was when I was 14, in 1967. Within the space of a few months, I was transferred twice, and ended up at the Special Unit at Red Bank, Newton-Le-Willows. It was a children's prison. High concrete wall with barbed wire. Locks on the cell doors and bars at the windows. Escape proof. I got away from there three times'.
'You're proud of that?'.
'Being in prison doesn't stop you from wanting to be outside of prison'.

She brought out a packet of cigarettes, extracted one and lit it up. 'Have a smoke', she said, tossing one over to me.

'Yes, I knew I was doing wrong. I'm not proud of that. Sometimes I'd admit to having taken things, when I hadn't. This let the people whose houses I'd broken into claim extra insurance. One lad at Edmund Castle[2] had a visit from his parents, who asked him to find someone to break into their house, so they could claim the insurance . . . '

'And did you?'

'Nope. Somebody else probably did, though. But there's many a time I've admitted breaking into houses that I hadn't broken into . . . I'd get them TIC'd[3] so that the police could clear them from their books. Once I was picked up by the police in Purley, near Croydon—a couple of years ago. They asked me to put my hands up to scores of break-ins, in that area; these were duly TIC'd and put down to me. No-one was interested, that I'd only been in Purley an hour or two, before I was picked up. The break-ins had been happening while I was banged-up in Red Bank . . .'

'I've heard of that happening'.

'With kids it happens a lot'.

'What led up to your present situation? What did you get life for?'

'That's a question I would really like to know myself. OK. It started in 1969. I was on the run from Red Bank. I broke into three houses in the Preston area. I didn't find out until afterwards, that the houses belonged to policemen. One was an assistant chief constable. Another was a uniformed inspector from the Fulwood district. The third wasn't a policeman, but he had a friend who was in CID. The inspector from Fulwood told me, before I was sent back to Red Bank, that if I was ever seen in Preston again I'd be for it . . . '

'He told you that?'

'He told me my feet wouldn't touch the ground. Right, well I didn't think much of it at the time. Until I was arrested for this GBH and aggravated burglary. The night I was arrested, I'd been walking through Preston in the early evening. It was cold, and I'd been walking around the streets trying to keep warm. I went to the bus station for a while, and left it at around half-nine. I went to a shop and bought some fish and chips, with the small amount of money I had. By ten o'clock I

---

[2] An approved school

[3] Taken into consideration when sentenced for other offences. 'Prison write-offs' still continue, to the extent that official statistics treat them as a separate category when dealing with crimes cleared up. Some police forces resist the approach, but with funding tied to performance other areas pursue it with vigour. Burglary, with low detection rates, was always a prime candidate.

was searching for shelter. I came across an office block, which was deserted. I broke in and went to sleep on the floor of one of the offices. I woke-up in the early hours feeling ill; I had a bad headache and a sore throat. The place wasn't heated or anything and it was chilly. I was very hungry and thirsty. I felt I wasn't able to carry on by myself, so every time I saw a car go by outside, I tried to attract attention, by turning the office light on and off. Am I talking too fast . . . ?'

She looked at her watch. 'You're alright for a while yet. Don't worry about talking too fast, I can keep up'.

'Well, I stayed by the window until I saw a police car go by. I switched the light on and off again, and waved to the policemen in the car; they stopped and I opened the window, and called out that I'd broken in and that I wanted to give myself up. The time must have been around three o'clock in the morning. Shortly afterwards a van load of policemen arrived and I was taken to Preston police station. When they got me there, they put me in a cell and my clothes were taken off me. A short time later, the door opened and a bobby tossed my clothes back at me, and told me to put them on. In place of my jeans was a pair of black trousers and my jacket was missing. I asked the copper, what was the score with my jacket and jeans, and he said I'd get them back when they were finished with them. I was brought out of the cell and made to sit at a table and a lot of uniformed policemen crowded around me. Well, I was scared man, I knew something wasn't right . . . I didn't think I'd be getting all that attention just because I'd broken into an office-block. A policeman came into the room . . . it was the same inspector whose house I'd broken into!'

'The one from . . . where? Fulwood?'

'That's right. As soon as I saw him, I knew I was going to be in big trouble. The first thing he said was "Forget about a solicitor" . . . I told him I was sorry I'd broken into his house, but he just reminded me of the warning he'd given me, and that it was my bad luck that I chose to ignore it. I asked if my parents could be told that I'd been arrested, but he said nobody was going to notify anyone. He took me back to the cell and locked me in. I'm certain that his remarks had been overheard by the other coppers, but no one ever said anything, then or afterwards, Bastards. Sorry. Anyway'.

• • •

'After another short while, I was unlocked again and taken to an interview room. Two CID officers were there. One of them said he was from Liverpool. He took a photograph from a small wallet and showed it to me. It was a black and white picture of me talking to a man I recognised . . . This next bit is very interesting. You'll like this . . . The year before I had gone to the Soviet Embassy in London to try to find out details of where my grandparents—my father's Mom and Dad—were living. I'd had the idea that they had lived in a city called Odessa in the Ukraine until just before that time, but they had been moved somewhere else. This was something I'd overheard, from a visitor to my home in Nelson, an elderly woman, who was the mother of a man called Max Simonenko . . . He was a friend of my father's and lived in the next street. Max and his family are Russian. Max's mother came to visit her son every year, from her home in Russia. On these occasions she, Max, Max's wife Elena and their daughter Nina would come to our home to talk and drink. Often, we would visit Max's house . . . My mother's parents died in the early 'sixties . . . '

'Your mother is English isn't she?'
'Yes. After they died, I believed I had no more grandparents. When I heard Max telling my father that his (my father's) parents were still alive, it was the first I knew of me having other grandparents. I wanted to write to them but Max said they'd been moved, and no longer lived in the same city. At the Embassy I was asked my business by a woman who went off to find one of the staff to talk to me. The man whom I saw next was, he said, a counsellor, introducing himself as Igor. Because it was late in the morning and just into the lunch-hour, he took me outside to a small garden where we sat at a bench, and talked for around half an hour. He had a paper bag, with some sandwiches or pastries in it, and he offered me some. I said no. I told him I wanted to trace my grandparents, and gave him the information I had, of their whereabouts. I wasn't very solid, because there wasn't much to go on. However, he said he'd make enquiries, and said I should contact him again in a few weeks' time. I should ask for him by name, Counsellor Igor Laptev, which I wrote down on a cigarette packet . . . During the brief time I spent with him, the conversation took in a few more subjects, but all innocent, mainly questions about where exactly my father came from, when did he come to England, was he in full employment. He seemed interested to know that I was hoping to become a writer one-day. It was a conversation which was as innocent as that. What I didn't know was that we were being photographed'.

I lit up another smoke.

'So the CID copper was showing me a black and white photograph. It showed me and the counsellor from the Embassy, talking to each other.

The copper asked me what we'd talked about. So I told him, but he wouldn't have it. He said he didn't believe me, and suggested Laptev had given me either a verbal or written message to be passed to someone in the ethnic communities in Nelson or Burnley . . . '

'Are there a lot of ethnic people living there?'

'What? Nelson and Burnley? Sure. Nelson has another name, it's known by, "Little Moscow". Maybe that says it all. Anyway, I'd told the CID bloke that what he was saying was ridiculous. I'd been just turned 17 when I visited the Embassy—was he trying to say that I was a spy or something? He began to insist that his version was true. What was it I'd written down before I left the Embassy? I said it was Laptev's name and the instructions he'd given me to contact him in a few months' time. Which I had not done, as it turned out . . . Had I passed anything on to my father? Or to anyone else? The Simonenkos (he knew their name and he knew that they were visitors to my father's house . . . !) All I could do was to keep denying what they were saying. He said that I was involved in something extremely serious and that my Dad was also involved. They were going to arrest him and "send him back to where he came from". I became upset. He said I would have to be put away somewhere for a while, maybe a couple of years, until they'd had time to sort it all out. I was going to be charged with burglary. I was to listen carefully to what the police told me, and I was to do as I was told. Otherwise they would have no option but to arrest my father....!'

• • •

'So I was taken back to the main room, and made to sit at a table. The inspector from Fulwood was there drinking tea, with some other plainclothes policemen. The inspector told me I had burgled a house in the night, and that I was going to be charged with aggravated burglary and GBH. One of the detectives was typing-out a document. I was told to sign it and was warned again that if I did not my father would be arrested and deported. The document was a "confession". It was written in a kind of language I've never used. A broad Lancastrian dialect. I wasn't told that the occupiers of that house I was supposed to have burgled had made a statement in which the attacker had been seen and described as "A thirty year-old man with black, curly hair" . . . The police could see full well that I wasn't responsible for the crime, but nobody said anything, none of the coppers questioned anything . . . !'

I explained that the inspector took me outside and put me in a car, which he drove towards the house he said had been burgled. It was still dark, so it must have been around five o'clock in the morning. I was in the back of the car in handcuffs. He stopped the car outside the door of a house which seemed to be the gable-end of a row of terraces. A few people were standing outside the door. The inspector wound his window down and shouted 'We've got the bastard!'—and then drove off before any of the people could actually see me.

He stopped the car again and told me to get out. We were a short distance away from the house. I got out and he told me to follow him into some back gardens or allotments. Then he produced a torch and shone it around briefly, then bent down and stood up again. He had a knife in his hand. He gave it to me and said 'Recognise it?' Because of the handcuffs I held it with difficulty and dropped it. I said I didn't recognise it. He said 'You should do, because it's yours'.

I told him it wasn't mine but he picked it up and said 'Yes it is. It is now!'

The woman had been listening carefully all the while. I'd been so wrapped up in what I was saying, bringing images back and describing them, that I'd almost forgotten where I was, or that she was there. She rubbed her eyes with her thumb and forefinger and asked me if I was saying I was fitted-up.

'Yes. Anyone looking into it closely will see that. I didn't understand the whole of what was going down, and I still don't. I reckon that the Preston police wanted me put away, perhaps for personal reasons. The police inspector, who conducted the proceedings, wanted me put away for breaking into his house. Also I had broken into the assistant chief constable's house and the house of a friend of another policeman in Preston. In itself that was enough reason to want me sent down. Enough bias. I'd been warned, that if I was seen in Preston again my feet "wouldn't touch the ground" ... Something else which bothers me, and may sound absurd, is the possibility that the set-up had begun ages ago ... it's bloody odd that the two policemen from Liverpool—they were Special Branch—could have arrived at Preston police station so soon after I had been taken to the station. If it was so serious, this political crap that started with me going to the Embassy, it may be that I'd been kept under some kind of surveillance myself. What I'd like to know is, if that's true, was I under surveillance before and up to the time I broke into the office block ... ? Was the burglary done by someone from Special Branch? Again, someone in that house got a clear look at the burglar, and described him in a witness statement ... I was not put on an identity parade and none of the occupiers of the house appeared in court, even as observers. If they had, they would have seen me, and known straightaway that I wasn't the burglar. By getting me to accept responsibility for the crime, and plead guilty, it meant that there was no examination of the witness statement or of any of the other so-called "evidence" in open court!'

The woman was silent for a while. I knew the whole thing was unbelievable. Except that in my own mind I knew it was true.
'I think I need some time to digest all that'.

CHAPTER THREE

Back in my cell, I wondered what had made me come out with it all. I'd told her things that maybe I shouldn't have. If the police should discover that I had told anyone about my allegations concerning the frame, and the nature of it, then it may be that they'd forget about me. I couldn't believe that they would let me go through a life sentence . . .

• • •

I had a short conversation with Will. He was two cells away and the only way I could talk to him was through the window. I put my table beneath the window and stood on it.

'Will!' I yelled. No answer. I called again. This time, a response.
'Yeah?'
'Who's that woman who does the interviews, is she probation or a psychologist or what?'
'Psychologist I think. Why?'
'She saw me this afternoon, I was in there for an hour, lots of questions'.
'You got to be careful what you say. Was she writing anything down?'
'No'.
'That don't mean anything. Some of them have tape-recorders in their drawers . . . '
'You're joking'.
'Course I'm not. You'll see'.

I climbed back down and sat on the cot for a think. In a way I'd been relieved to bring everything out, as I had that afternoon at the interview . . . I felt that somebody ought to know where I was coming from. Additionally, it was a relief to get it all out. Maybe the woman could do something . . . but she never did and I was never called up by her again.

Later that evening at eight o'clock the cell door was opened and a screw asked me for my clothes. He had a large cardboard box to put them in. He also put my plastic cutlery into the box, and my pen—a Bic biro. The box was left out on the landing outside my door to be reclaimed the following morning. The red night-light was switched on at ten o'clock. No one brought the Mogadon I'd supposedly been written-up for. I couldn't sleep. After an hour or so I got a newspaper and put it over my face, the darkness was wonderful and I was fast asleep within minutes. But the night's events hadn't stopped yet. There was more to come. At midnight I was woken by a loud banging on the cell door. It was the night screw.

'Take that newspaper away from your face!', he said.
'Look boss, I can't sleep with this red light on. It's keeping me awake. If it's got to stay on the only way I can sleep is with the newspaper shutting out the light . . . '
'I've got to check that you're still there. Don't put that newspaper over you face again or you'll find yourself nicked in the morning'.

Incredible! I knew I was going to be happy. I rolled a smoke and wondered what the next day would bring. First thing next morning, I saw the landing officer, and put down sick. He asked me why I wanted to see the doctor, but I told him it was personal. A couple of hours later I was seen by the doc.

'Morning doctor. I was written up for something to help me sleep yesterday but it wasn't issued. Can you tell me why?'
'You should have been given something last night . . . leave it with me, and I'll have a word with the dispensary later on'.

Back on the wing, I was told that I couldn't go out for exercise because I'd been seeing the doctor when the exercise was on. I said I needed some fresh air and some exercise, but I got nowhere. It was quickly becoming apparent that my daily programme was dictated by the whim of the screws. I'd been told that exercise was not a privilege but a right—providing the weather was not inclement. But because exercise was perceived as a 'pleasurable' activity by the screws (!) the denying of it represented an element of punishment. I looked forward to the exercise periods, because they were the only occasions—save for brief moments at meal times—that I had to talk to Will and Phil. From then on I had to weigh carefully whether or not a necessary application (to see the doctor, governor, probation officer or the librarian for example) was worth missing out on the exercise.

● ● ●

A fortnight after I arrived at Walton, there was a slight improvement. I was asked if I wanted to work. I was told that I could go into the prison laundry if I wanted. The job was helping to operate one of the giant colanders. After certain items—such as bedsheets or tablecloths—had been in the washing machines and spin dryers, my job was to feed them into the colanders for pressing. It was hot and sweaty work but it made the days go by faster than being banged-up in the cell. The weekly pay was pittance. Just enough to purchase half an ounce of tobacco, a packet of cigarette papers and a box of matches. To be given a proper wage in proportion to the amount of work we provided would detract from the punishment ethos. People were sent to prison to be punished.

The reformist argument that a prisoner's punishment was his removal from society, the loss of his freedom, was regarded as a namby-pamby notion. People were sent to prison to *be* punished.

Will was also working in the laundry. His job was to operate three large spin dryers. One day he was given the sack and transferred to another prison. I learned the ins and outs of it almost straight away. One of the other lads, a long-termer, had devised a plan to escape. His idea was to hide in one of the spin dryers, just before everybody was taken back to the wing, at the end of the day. As soon as the workshop was clear, he intended to emerge from the drier and break through the skylight, onto the laundry roof. From there he would make his way, along the roof, to an area that was close enough to the outside wall, to make an escape possible. Unfortunately there was a roll count before we left the laundry. This meant that the screws knew there was a body missing and that the only place he could be was somewhere in the laundry. When everyone else had been taken back to the wing, the screws went into the laundry with dogs. The lad was caught in his hiding place and he was taken down to the punishment block.

Because Will was the operator of the spin dryers, it was assumed that he was in collusion with the escapee. Half an hour later Will was with Phil and myself, as we went to collect our tea.

'Might be ghosted tonight', he told us.

Being 'ghosted' meant being suddenly transferred out of the prison. One day you're there and the next you'd disappeared. He told us the SP about the attempted escape. The next day, Will was gone.

Most of the talk between Phil and me was of escape. We knew that escape would have been impossible, there was too much security, but it didn't stop us thinking about it. Out on the exercise yard we would examine all of the options, spotting possible routes and looking for blind areas. It was a harmless enough bit of fantasising. Most people in prison do the same. Needless to say, we never actually tried it on.

Walton prison was a dirty and cheerless place in those days, in the early 'seventies. There were no toilet facilities in the cells and many of the cons were banged-up for most of the time. There were limited work options; working in the laundry, or sewing mailbags, or breaking lead cables open for the copper inside.

There was an education department, but it was not very well organized.

• • •

A few months after I arrived at Walton I was transferred to the hospital section. I was having tremendous difficulty accepting my lot, because I knew that it was not deserved. By that time I'd been pretty well briefed about the life sentence and I knew that—unless something happened to put a halt to it—I was likely going to serve ten or eleven years. The prospect of that was disturbing. Gone was my hope that the police would honour their side of the bargain. Yet my father hadn't been deported. That was something.

The hospital was a large and relatively modern part of the prison, and the cells were large and well aired. My cell had a big sash window which let in lots of sunshine and there was a radio facility on the wall. I listened a lot to Radio 2.

One day I went for a shower and one of the other men was there; he had breasts like a woman and was apparently awaiting a sex change. It was made more incongruous because he was a big, burly geezer built like a heavyweight boxer . . . I couldn't figure out where he was coming from. If he had the sex change he would still look the same and there was no way he could ever have been mistaken for a woman. I watched him deteriorate into a zombie-like state, perhaps because of the drugs he was on. He would shuffle along in slow motion, taking long minutes to cover a distance of only a few feet. I guess he was sent to a mental hospital eventually.

I enjoyed the quiet of the hospital section. I spent most of the time reading, devouring book after book mainly because it stopped me thinking too much. A screw came to see me one day and asked if I wanted to appeal against my sentence. He asked if I wanted any help with it and I told him that I did. I was shown a form, which asked the following questions:

Do you wish to appeal against conviction?
Do you wish to appeal against sentence?
Do you want leave to appeal?

I answered 'Yes' to each question. On the reverse side of the form was a space in which I should have made out a list of my grounds for appealling. The screw said I should just write down what I wanted to say, and so I wrote a brief statement claiming that the police had manufactured evidence; but even as I was writing it, I wondered whether I was creating trouble for my dad.

The appeal failed. Really, I should've had it drawn up by a solicitor, who knew what he was doing. There had already been talk that my sentence constituted a miscarriage, in any event, because the two life sentences were far too savage a sentence, for the crimes of GBH and aggravated burglary. Evidently!

I gave up all hope of justice. I wasn't from a wealthy family and couldn't afford to pay solicitor's fees, or a private detective, or an investigative journalist, to dig into my case. The only hope that existed was that the person who was really responsible for the burglary would either be caught or give himself up. But there seemed little chance of either. I knew that a description of him existed, because it was there in the witness statements from the householders.

While in the hospital I was seen by Dr Gray, from Grendon Prison in Buckinghamshire. He wanted me to go to Grendon. He said that he was concerned, that I may try to kill myself. I *had* thought about killing myself, this was true. The feelings I had were awful. I was upset for most of the time, because I couldn't accept my sentence, considering that it was unjust.

• • •

I understood that I was being punished in the most severe way that the courts allowed. That punishment was, by definition, inflicting harm (otherwise it would not be punishment); it was the case that I was being harmed in the most severe way. Naturally, I wanted to have an end to it. Perhaps the only thing that stopped me from ending things permanently was the resolve to have the mistake brought out into the open one day—regardless of how long that would take.

The people who had stitched me up would have to account for it eventually . . . but if I were not there, they would get away with it. I told Doctor Gray that I would like to go to Grendon. But I lied to him. I wanted Grendon for the wrong reasons. Its relaxed regime was well known, and I wanted my prison experience to be as painless as possible . . . I wanted the level of harm to be reduced, and made bearable. I had no intention of wanting group therapy. I agreed to Grendon, because it represented a soft option.

• • •

Soon after my twentieth birthday, I was transferred out of Walton. Five screws came to collect me in the morning. Before leaving the gaol I was handcuffed to two of them and bundled into a prison van. Two more screws sat in the back, and one up front next to the driver. I thought I was on my way to Grendon. I thought it was odd that the screws wouldn't tell me where I was going . . . out on the motorway I saw that we were heading across country towards Yorkshire! I knew that we were not travelling South, but assumed they were going to pick up someone else, who was down for Grendon.

We reached Wakefield and within 15 minutes arrived at Wakefield gaol . . . I knew that Wakefield was an adult prison and a 'dispersal'. I breathed a sigh of relief, because I was not an adult prisoner, so the likelihood was that we were making a pick-up, before continuing South. I was taken out of the van and the handcuffs removed in reception. One of the reception screws, grinning widely, said 'Welcome to Wakefield . . . '

I thought there was something wrong here. What was going on? I was not an adult prisoner. I had the presence of mind not to get into an argument then and there, because there was no way that any of the screws had the authority required, to redress the situation.

The best I could do was petition the Home Office or write to my MP later on. Meanwhile I would ask to see the governor at the earliest opportunity.

Wakefield was one of the gaols that were built in the Victorian age, a dark and shadowy place. It held around 350 to 400 captives, two thirds of whom were serving life sentences for murder. The remainder were all serving sentences of five years or over. All were regarded as long-termers. The cells were all single cells, and different from Walton, in that more latitude was allowed to the prisoners in the furnishing of them. Rugs and curtains were allowed. Radios and vacuum flasks were allowed. Cell hobbies, too. It was an amazing feature of the place, that each inmate was permitted to have certain tools in his possession, these included small screwdrivers and Stanley knives. It was incomprehensible to me. These people were segregated from the world outside because of their dangerousness and yet inside the prison they were considered to be safe enough to each other for them to be allowed articles which were certainly dangerous weapons!

Most of the inmates had tremendous image problems. These were men who had been convicted of the most serious crimes. In a prison such as Wakefield, the only thing that was truly respected was violence. This meant that the more violent someone was deemed to be the more respect that was given. Weak people were trodden down, and made into 'Joeys', rather like the fag system in public schools. Their lives were made intolerable. There was always a way of escape for the fag, but not for the Joey, because the Joey wasn't going anywhere, except where he was, for many years.

In the outside world it's very rare to meet a murderer. Most people, I'm sure, are very thankful for that. If there was a high-rise block of flats, containing 300 killers and social misfits it would be a place to avoid at all costs. Prisons are not much different. They are communities of people just the same, except, of course, they are the kind of people who no ordinary person in his or her right mind would want anything to do with. And once in with them, there was no escape. The primary observation I was to make of the murderers was that most of them regarded themselves as superior people; for them, to take a life was the ultimate ego trip. This wasn't true of all of them, but it was of the majority. Inside prison, they still regarded themselves as superior to everyone else, and took great pains to project the image of violence.

A weak person stood no chance, living in close proximity to them. The weakest were the first to be singled out and persecuted. From then on, the weak person lived in fear. The measure of inflicted harm, of punishment, was far greater for the weaker inmate than it was for the stronger one. People have tried to figure out why people commit suicide in prison. Some point to conditions and make the case that, if the conditions are improved, it will help to stop the suicides . . . but the conditions of a place have little to do with it; bullies in the school playground are one thing, but in prison—whether or not the prison is a progressive, modern one—the bullies threaten to kill.

Most prison suicides are of weak and immature people who have to cope with fear and torment. Little wonder that they seek a route to be rid of it. As for myself, I was not a particularly strong character. Certainly I was not in the league of the 'Faces'—those who ran the prison by intimidation. It was only a matter of time, I thought, before I would be leaned on myself. Perversely, the fact that I had been put on the A-List was in itself a degree of protection because, in the prison hierarchy, a Category A man was at the very top, respected the most. I learned that although there were many very dangerous men in Wakefield at that time, very few were Category A. A handful, no more.

The fact that I was among that small number seemed totally wrong. The Home Office's view of me must have been influenced by completely erroneous information. Again, this did not add up. How could a youth of 18, convicted of GBH and aggravated burglary, be perceived as a threat to society?—even had I done the crime. My own belief was that a mistake had certainly been made, and it was a mistake, on such a scale, that it had to be covered up. The visit I made to the Soviet Embassy, and the subsequent turn of events, had to be the key. But I didn't know what could be done about it. The whole of it was so bloody well implausible . . . but who would just take my word for it?

CHAPTER FOUR

I'd been warned a few times that some of the 'hard' cases would eventually try it on with me. These were the ones who controlled the tobacco. Who lent it out and charged extra when it was returned—the so-called 'Tobacco Barons'. I wasn't a 'tough guy', nor did I belong to any particular clique. More than this, I was naturally quiet and, I thought, unassuming. My wages, such as they were, were enough to keep me going in tobacco, through careful budgeting. I didn't borrow. Although I didn't know it then, it was these conditions which made me stand out from the others—so as to make me a target.

● ● ●

When the attack came it was when I least expected it. I'd gone to the recess, to fetch a bowl of hot water for a wash. As I was putting the bowl on the table in my cell, I sensed someone behind me. I started to turn around but I was too late. I felt an arm go around my throat, and the press of sharp metal at the side of my neck.

'Just keep you mouth shut', I heard a voice say, 'or I'll cut your fucking throat'.
'Hit him over the head! Knock the bastard out!'

I felt someone else undoing my jeans and pulling them down. I knew then what was going to happen, but I couldn't believe it. There were four of them. All the while I was held around my neck. I couldn't move at all. The chiv[1] was kept at my throat. The pain I felt as each one raped me was excruciating. The one who'd had hold of my neck let go and immediately one of the others grabbed my hair while he had his turn. I couldn't see anything because I was held face down across the cot.

'You tell anyone about this and you're dead. We'll plunge you. You understand . . . ?'
'Plunge the bastard anyway'.
'Not worth it. He ain't gonna grass us, are you son?'

Again I felt the point of the knife.

'Cos he knows what'll happen if he does. Right?'

---

[1] Prison slang for knife or blade

I didn't say anything. I was looking into darkness. My mind was a million miles away, and my body was that distance behind. Everything that was relevant had just died. Blank.

The cell door was slammed shut. I couldn't sleep that night. I asked again what I'd done to be in such a place. I knew that I wasn't going to survive. No way. How could it be possible? What was I going to do? Out came the razor blade and it was put to my veins . . . the temptation to end everything there and then was so strong. But I saw the faces of my family—they'd never know why I'd done it. And I thought it was important that people knew.

Next morning, Jack knocked on my cell door. I'd put a wedge of wood under the door, to stop it from being opened.

'It's me, Jack'.

I got up and pulled the wedge away. Jack came in.

'You not havin' no breakfast?'

I wanted him to go away. I didn't want anything more than to be left alone.

'They shouldn't have sent you here Alex'.

I didn't say anything. I was sat on the cot with my eyes closed.

'But they did. It's my birthday tomorrow. I'll be 21'.
'Well'. He rolled a couple of smokes and lit them. 'Here, have a smoke'.
'I don't feel too good Jack. I've had a bad night. Not much sleep . . . '
'Sure. Listen, I know what happened yesterday man'.
'What d'you mean?'
'It's all over the wing. Summat like that ain't kept a secret'.
'Ah, shit'.
'What're you gonna do?'
'Dunno'.
'Well have a think. What are your options, man?'
'I can't go to the screws and grass. I've got to live here'.
'That's right Alex. No grassing. Good'.
'I didn't even see them Jack!'
'No?'
'I don't want it to happen again . . . but it will, won't it?'

'Look'. He sat down on the chair, and leaned his arms on the table. 'You can't go to the screws. Even if you did they won't do owt, I mean you didn't even see who they were. OK. Listen. This is serious . . . if you leave it, and I hate to say it, but if you leave it it'll probably happen again and you don't want that. So you got to do something. All right, I'll tell you this. I've heard a whisper. We—that's me and a few of my mates—reckon we know one of the geezers who did it. He's done the same thing before. Now we ain't a hundred per cent sure, so I'm not gonna give you his name just yet. But we'll find out. And as soon as we do I'll come back to you. In the meantime, wedge-up again, and read a book or something. See you later'.

•   •   •

Jack didn't come back that day or the day after. I didn't stay shut up behind my door, as he'd suggested, but I was wary of who came near me. I'd been sick three or four times and had to empty the bucket down the sluice. Some of the cons were giving me odd looks, but nobody came near me. I had a visit on my birthday; my mom had come all the way from Nelson to see me. She brought me a birthday card which said 'TWENTY-ONE TODAY! KEY TO THE DOOR!'.

She asked me if I was well and I said I was. I didn't want to say anything that'd upset her. She said that I'd to stay out of trouble, and it wouldn't be long now before I was out. I didn't say what I really thought; that I wouldn't be home for a long time yet. After the visit I went back to the wing, and thought of my mom travelling all the way back. She never travelled well, and was usually travelsick if she went too far. She had to use either buses or trains, because she doesn't drive a car.

•   •   •

It was to be a couple of days before Jack came to my cell again.

'OK Alex, we have a name. He was definitely one of the bastards who attacked you; we know, because he's been overheard braggin' about it. So, you don't want it to happen again, yeh? The only thing you can do, is give him a hiding then. Are you any good with your fists?'
'I don't know Jack. I haven't had many fights. A couple'.
'Alright, well here's the geezer's name'.

He told me who it was and where I could find him. He had a cell on the Fours, the highest landing. He would be in at a certain time.

'It's up to you now. I'll see you man. Oh, one more thing—he's likely to be tooled-up so be careful. Use this'. He pulled a metal tube from inside the sleeve of his jacket. 'See you'.

I hefted the metal tube in my hand. It wasn't particularly heavy but I knew I wouldn't like being on the wrong end of it . . . I went up the stairs to the Fours with my heart in my mouth. I couldn't believe I was doing this, but every step I took became one step nearer the bastard who had used me, and who, if I didn't do something about it, would more than likely do it to me again. Also, if *I* didn't sort it out others would try it.

Outside his cell I heard voices. Very quietly, I opened the cover on the spy-hole in his door and saw that he was having sex with one of the other cons. So I went down to the Threes recess, and sat in there for half-an-hour or so. Then I went back. Again I quietly peered through the spy-hole, and I saw that he was alone. I pulled the metal tube from the waistband of my jeans, and pushed the cell door wide open. He saw me and clocked the tube in my hand; he made a frantic grab for a heavy PP9 battery which served as one of the most common weapons used by cons (usually it is slid into a sock and used as a kind of mace), but I got to him before he could pick it up.

I gave him a few whacks with the metal bar. Afterwards I was told that his screams could be heard in every part of the prison. As I was hitting him, I was absurdly conscious that I shouldn't hit him too hard. I guess I could've gone over the top. Really, I should've laid right into him, but I couldn't. I had felt disgusted after the attack on me, but it was disgust for the men who had done what they had to me . . . but as I was hearing the con screaming I guess I felt a disgust at myself. I left his cell and put the metal tube down outside his door. Screws were piling up the stairs and along the landing . . . I stayed where I was and leaned on the landing rail waiting for them.

They took hold of me and marched me off down the block. The next day I was brought before the governor. I was asked what my reason was for doing as I did, but I couldn't grass. Then I was sentenced to 56 days in solitary.

● ● ●

The sentence was served down the block. My cell was bare during daylight hours, save for a tree-stump which served as a chair. At eight o'clock every evening I was allowed to bring a cot into the cell to sleep on. This would be removed the next day, before breakfast. I was not permitted to smoke, of course, but the night watchman would slip me a couple of cigarettes and matches under the door. I was not treated badly by the block staff, and I guess it was the first time I realised that not all screws were bad; there were good ones too. This was to be an important realisation. When I had exercise it was in my own. On my first exercise, I had to be taken through the main prison to the exercise area. Other cons were calling,

'Well done mate!' and 'You should've hit the bastard harder!'

Jack saw me almost every day . . . he'd managed to get me smokes and matches—taking risks. If he'd got caught he'd have been for it. The governor, during his daily rounds, would stop and talk for a while. I knew he was aware of the circumstances of my actions, although he never said so. It was there, in the way he spoke to me . . . one day he said I could have a table in the cell and a chair to sit on. He brought me books and pens, pencils and paper.

After I had been in the block for a week or so he asked me if I wanted to work. I didn't have to, he said, but it might help me get through the days. I agreed, and a load of sacking was delivered to be made up into mailbags. I'd sit there sewing mailbags and daydream. All of my dreams were of things I'd done before my arrest. Good things. Sometimes I'd dream about what I wanted to do in the future then I'd realise I had no future—and I'd accidentally stab myself with the needle.

A lot of the time was spent wondering what I could do to get my liberty back . . . but for that I'd need people who believed in me. There wasn't much chance of that. When my 56 days were up, the governor told me he couldn't risk me attacking the man again. He put me on Rule 43, GOAD.[2] It was almost the same as being down the block except the cot could be kept in the cell all day. In addition, I found that I'd amassed a substantial mound of back-pay (which I wouldn't have got if I'd refused the mailbags), so I was alright for tobacco. I was content enough. It also appeared that I'd acquired a reputation, becoming one of 'the faces'—which made me wonder at the incongruity of life. Two months earlier I'd been ready to use a razor blade on myself . . . I was never to be bothered by another con again.

• • •

The clock had turned 1974. Outside my cell window I could see the top of some trees on the other side of the perimeter wall. Every day I'd watch as the leaves gradually fell off them, until they were bare and

---

[2] Good order and discipline

stark. There was a pigeon, caught in a roll of the razor wire, which embroidered the tops of the walls and fences. I thought that the screws would try to free it, but it was still there weeks later, a raggedy bundle of empty feathers. The thought struck me that the pigeon hadn't done anything wrong to go and die in a prison built for humans. Extreme pathos. Hurt. Nearer to my window, I watched workmen turn a derelict part of the prison into a construction site. The word had it that they were constructing a separate building, a security block, a prison within a prison.

I wasn't to see it finished, however, because the screws came and told me to get my things packed . . . I was being transferred out. This time I knew we were headed South. I asked the screws in the van which prison I was going to, and they told me it was Grendon. I must have heaved one hell of a sigh of relief.

Grendon prison accepted me, in spite of the fact that I was a Category A prisoner. I was told on arrival that there would be no restrictions on my movements and that I wouldn't be treated any differently from anyone else. The regime was structured around a specific treatment policy, involving group therapy and remedial programmes designed to help prisoners with behavioural problems. These problems involved anything from alcoholism and compulsive gambling to much more serious crimes, such as rape and murder. It was the only prison in the country that worked to such design, and there was a waiting list for vacant places.

I knew that I was going there for the wrong reasons, that is, not because I needed the therapy, but because of the relaxed regime. Because of this, I couldn't help feeling guilt; with the knowledge that I was taking up space that another guy needed a lot more than I did. I didn't last long there. One of the fundamental requirements of a prisoner at Grendon is to accept and come to terms with his offence. That was something I couldn't do. After two months or so I asked to be transferred out, but I was told that it wasn't possible.

Apparently I had to wait for another three months before it could be arranged, and to my thinking that was too long. I began to look for ways to get myself moved. There was only one possibility. I had to break the rules somehow, so that the issue could be forced. It had to be a harmless device, and one which would cause the minimum trouble for others. In the end I thought I'd found a way.

I went into my landing recess, and removed all the metal handles from the mop buckets. I took them back to my cell and bent them into a hook. Then I tore a bedsheet into strips and wound them around my waist with the hook attached. This done, I went out on exercise and when I was sure that a screw was looking my way I ducked behind a workshop, and legged it a couple of hundred yards towards a corner of the perimeter wall, and then stopped and waited for the screws to catch up. That was it. I was put in front of the Board of Visitors, charged with being out of bounds or something. I explained why I'd done it, and my reasons were accepted. I was awarded a token punishment and taken to Winchester prison the next day, to serve out the punishment down the block. That done, the screws came for me, and told me I was being moved to Albany prison on the Isle of Wight . . . On the way there we had to use the ferry from Portsmouth. The van was driven into the vehicle hold . . . it was the first time I'd been in a ship and, woof, the last if that experience was anything to go by. I was handcuffed-up to one of the van's barred windows; I wasn't allowed to get out, and the hold was full of diesel fumes, from the lines of cars and lorries . . . we were rolling around in that dark place, and my stomach wasn't where it ought to be.

'We'll be out of here soon', one of the screws said.
'What happens if we sink, then, boss', I asked, indicating the window bar I was 'cuffed to.
'Well, you'll be well fucked'.
'I hope we don't sink then'.

•   •   •

Albany was the sort of prison where even an A-man could wander around, like the rest of the cons. It was (and remained until recently) a maximum security 'dispersal' gaol, located just across the road from the more notorious Parkhurst. Prisoners around the country who'd had the misfortune to spend time at either prison referred to them as one unit, 'The Island'. When I arrived there, Albany had no outer wall as such, but there were two 18 feet high fences, each of which carried a double row of razor wire (now banned by the European Convention). Between the two fences, was a narrow strip of land, officially the 'sterile area', a no-man's land—with the inner fence wired-up to trigger an alarm system if touched by anything heavier than a pigeon.

Dog-handlers with alsations patrolled both sides of the perimeter fences, and at night Albany was lit-up like Heathrow, from great high floodlight stanchions, with clusters of ultra bright electric lights, branching from the tops of them. The intensive nature of the security system was considered enough to contain the inmates, which meant that the cons were able to socialise between wings and to associate together out on the exercise field and during evening association every day without being closely supervised by the screws. More than this, all the cell doors were operated electronically, and were opened and locked, by a burglar[3] sitting in a central control room. The burglar could see each cell on the wing by way of video monitors mounted on each landing.

During the night, if anyone wanted a shower, or felt ill, or wanted to visit the toilet, the burglar could be contacted via an intercom system that was fitted into every cell. There was sufficient suspicion that the intercoms remained 'live' after the cons switched them off to cause radio sets to be turned up whenever there was anything private to be discussed in the cells.

I was surprised in the reception area, because the orderly was a con I'd known in Wakefield prison. I remembered he'd been ghosted from there a few weeks before I'd been transferred out myself. His name was Vic and he came from London. He'd killed somebody in Leeds, so he'd had to start out his sentence in the north. When the screw had taken off my handcuffs, I went over to shake hands.

'Hello, Vic!'
'Stone the crows. Alex. Welcome to Disneyland!'

That must've been the first time I'd gone through a prison reception, and been given clothes that actually fitted me—together with a decent cup of tea. It always pays to have a pal working in reception. It does make life a lot easier.

'You're goin' on A-wing, mate. I'll see you up there, as soon as I get some free time. D'you wanna hand with the boxes?'

He was referring to the two cardboard boxes I'd brought with me, and which contained all my worldly possessions. They weren't heavy, so I told him I could manage.

'Don't go in the TV Room on the wing tonight Alex'.
'Why not?'
'The telly's goin' up . . . '

Before he could say more, one of the reception screws came to escort me up to A-wing, in the main prison. When I got to the wing, the reception screw left me standing outside the wing office. Inside, sat behind a table, was the PO.[4] He called me in and read out some of the prison's

---

[3] Cons term for a security screw
[4] Principal officer

rules. There was to be no red security light on in my cell at nights, nor would I be expected to leave my clothes outside my cell door, either. What he was saying, basically, was that there were facilities available to meet the long-termer's needs, and provided I played ball everything would be fine. This was the pep talk that all new arrivals were given.

'You'll find that this is a relaxed community. Very little trouble . . . '

A deafening explosion rocked the telephone on his table. There was a sound of glass shattering and people yelling. An ordinary blue-shirted officer, breathing heavily, appeared at the office door.

'They've blown the television up sir . . . '

'Right', said the PO, 'You get this lad to his cell. Hang about. In fact bang all the fuckers up!' The uniformed screws had four basic ranks. First there were the ordinary officers, who compared to a police constable, in that they were the most junior in rank. These screws knew more about the cons on their patch than anyone else, including the Home Office. I often heard it said that it was the screws that should be allowed to advise the prison administrators to the highest level, because they knew more about the running of their gaols than anybody else did. Next in seniority, was the SO, or senior officer, who compared to a police sergeant, and then there were the POs, principal officers, who compared to police inspectors. A PO was usually in charge of the running of a wing and was the senior officer on the wing.

The last of the uniformed ranks were the chief officers. They wore a lot of gold braid on their hats and were in charge of all the uniformed screws. A chief officer was afforded the most respect, both from other officers and from the cons themselves. They were the screws with the most experience, often having worked up from being an ordinary screw over a good number of years. The closest comparison to the chief would be the hospital matron. My experience of chief officers was a good one. They told you straight what they thought, and so you knew where you stood. If a con was genuinely interested in reforming himself, a chief would go a long way towards helping in that process. They were fair. In addition, the chief was the liaison officer and the link with the administration. He was listened to by the governors.

I can't remember who the chief at Albany was, because I wasn't there for very long. Somebody put my name up as being involved in some scam or other and I was ghosted out within only a few months of my arrival. One of the cons I remember was George Davis, who maintained *his* innocence. He was lucky, because he had a strong campaign going on the outside, to keep his name in the public arena. All over London the slogan 'George Davis is Innocent, OK?' appeared on walls and motorway bridges. I don't think he would've got out if it hadn't been for his friends on the outside. I heard later, that he'd been nicked again for another blag—and I was saddened because he wasn't a bad geezer.

• • •

I was fast becoming an underwater swimmer. Submerged by the system, I was learning now not to drown. But in the doing of it I was becoming known as a bit of a non-conformist. While people have said to me that it's good that I've kept my own identity and refused to become a robot, this fact hasn't earned me any friends in the Home Office. All lifers are supposed to adhere to a 'general behavioural pattern'—because all lifers are treated exactly the same; there isn't any room for individuality. To fight against it is seen as banging one's head against a brick wall. A favourite saying of the authorities is 'You can't beat the system'. But that's untrue. There *is* a way of beating the system. But if you can figure it out God help you, you won't be liked by the system for it.

The prison administrators and the civil servants at the Home Office point to a prisoner and say 'If you can't handle life in here, how are you going to cope when you get out?'—as though there was any similarity at all between the two worlds: on the one hand the supremely abnormal world of captivity; and on the other hand the real world beyond the prison walls. Logically, the more one disowns the aberration—and this means struggling and fighting against it—the more attuned one becomes to the values and principles of the world outside.

It's simple enough to see the foolishness and fallibility of the administrators' argument. If they succeed in turning someone's mind to the extent of that person accepting the abnormal as normal, then there's little wonder that the prisoner concerned, upon returning to society, has lost touch with reality.

CHAPTER FIVE

I was moved out of Albany in a prison van, thinking I was going back up North, nearer home. So I was surprised when the journey lasted only five minutes . . . I'd been taken across the road—to Parkhurst. I didn't know it then, but this was to be my home for the next six years. The stories about Parkhurst were legend. I'd heard them told and re-told, ever since I started the sentence in Risley.

Five years earlier, Parkhurst had gone up, resulting in the worst prison riot so far seen in British penal history. The talk was of rivers of blood flowing down landings, and the making of a legend—Frankie Fraser. A geezer from London, the screws had tried to break him but he gave out as good as he got. He was overcome and eventually beaten. Literally. So he needed assistance, to get around for the next few months . . . But Frank's part in all that earned him universal respect from the country's prisoners. He ended up serving a long time, and all because of the Parkhurst riot.

My introduction to Parkhurst was F2, it's notorious hospital landing. There were maybe 20 or so cons on that landing, and all were either on heavy drugs or were waiting for Rampton or Broadmoor, because they'd been nutted off. I don't know if all lifers had to go on F2 when they arrived: I doubt it, but when I asked why I'd been put onto a medical landing, the screw said 'So the doctor can have a look at you'.

Oh. I didn't like the sound of that. That night, there was almost no kip, there were too many animals mooing and bleating. Next door on one side was a bloke who thought he was an owl, and on the other side a monkey. It was my first meeting with mentally ill prisoners. Some of them were cons that the system itself had driven mad. Next day, I was seen by a doctor. We prisoners all thought they were the pits. I remember one who could've been portrayed only by someone like Donald Pleasance or Jack Nicholson, in a role reversal from *One Flew Over The Cuckoo's Nest*. Having said that, the doctors and psychiatrists had considerable—sometimes, it seemed to us, complete—influence over the rest of the prison's administration.

When the doctor saw me enter his office he steepled his hands on the table in front of him and nodded to indicate a chair. After I'd sat down, and rolled up a smoke, I looked up to see him looking straight at me, as though I was something he'd never come across before. His glasses were distracting; they reflected small bright colour spots as the light hit them. He picked up my file, which was also on the table before him.

'So you're finding it hard to settle down?'

'I don't think it would be very healthy to "settle down" in prison . . . '

'You don't admit responsibility for your crime'.

'I don't admit responsibility because it wasn't my crime'.

'So you're very bitter'.

'Very upset'.

'Naturally'.

'Yes'.

'I'm putting you on C-wing. You'll like it on C-wing'.

• • •

The main prison at Parkhurst comprised four separate wings. These were A, B, C and D-wings. Of these only C-wing stuck out because it was understood to house psychotics and prisoners just back from Rampton and Broadmoor. C-wing was controlled by psychiatrists. It housed a maximum of 20 or so cons, although it had enough empty cells to house a hundred.

C-wing prisoners were not allowed to associate with cons from the other three wings. Apparently, C-wing was known as a specific treatment situation. There was one screw to every four cons; over on the 'main' it was more like one screw to every 20 cons. My first few days were spend adjusting to the regime and becoming familiar with both sets of laws, those of the screws and the laws of the prisoners themselves. I wasn't bothered by any of the other men. Only a couple of them went out of their way to speak . . . It was a case of gradually coming to know complex people, for each one was an individualist throwing many shadows.

I was eventually given work in the toy soldier shop, C-wing's only workshop. The job was to paint tiny toy soldiers, and animals with '00' brushes dipped in minute pots of colour. It wasn't work really, more occupational therapy. Inside the workshop, each con was motoring at his own pace; some got their work done fairly quickly, while others managed to paint only one toy soldier a day. Some would paint the soldiers the wrong colours. Everybody was on the same pay.

The Major was one of the first cons to say hello. He was a tall geezer, with an immense girth, a beer drinker's stomach. His flight deck was severely damaged, and this also affected his way of walking; it was the stagger of the man who's had too many ales. There was always a full jug of diesel, in his hand and it was a marvel to watch him weaving around so much, without spilling a drop of the tea. He spoke in short sentences, ending in exclamation marks, you could actually watch a sentence forming on his forehead, and hear it in words a while later.

'Givvus a kiss 'cos I wanna be sick, ugh!'

He was given a short home leave and before he went he came around the cells asking if any of us could tell him where to find a decent prostitute. One of the men told him they could be found walking on Brighton Pier in the afternoons. 'Course that was a lie. But The Major took it seriously, went to Brighton, and accosted a woman who was out for a walk along the pier. She screamed, and a policeman came and took him away. His home leave was terminated, and he was back on C wing the same day.

Another of the men I got to know was Bill. He was an old man with a life sentence; he'd been in Broadmoor for many years and now they'd kicked him out, to resume his sentence in prison. Bill knew he wasn't going to make it. He was old, and he had ailments. He was built like a stick. He was tired. Bill hardly spoke to anyone, but he'd talk to me sometimes. Bill had nice dreams, and the next day he'd be asking how much a barge or a caravan would cost. Although Bill was old and frail, he'd been a right villain in his day. Sometimes he would reveal a spark of anger. One day some of the other men were playing table tennis and they'd set the table up too near Bill's door, making too much noise. Bill came out of the cell and, to the players' astonishment, began to smash up the table tennis table. Bill went down to the treatment hatch and asked for a tot of Valium, then another tot of Valium, and by this time the screws were telling him he'd had too much to drink. Eventually, he made it back to his cell door, and went back inside and fell asleep.

There was Andy, a man who came from Whalley not very far from Nelson and Burnley. He'd killed his baby daughter and was three years into a life sentence. Another of the lifers, a man in his late thirties, was involved in some way with the Salvation Army and kept stacks of LPs with recordings of the various Citadel bands. His name was Keith. Whatever he'd done, it was obvious to everyone that he was paying for it; he'd often scream out during the night, and in the daytime it could be seen there in his face. Something was tormenting him. He was a quiet well-spoken man, and always had a good word for people. But, always, painful vibes. Nobby was another old guy who'd been lifed-up. He had a box of assorted spectacles on his table. they had different coloured lenses, and when you looked through them you could see a person's aura! He told me that once, when he was in Broadmoor, he was in the next room to another patient, who was dying.

He said the staff let him into the room with his tinted glasses, and actually witnessed the sight of the sound leaving the dying man's body.

He used to talk about immorality, and the 'Life Force'—I found it all very convincing, the way he told it. There was much about Nobby that was unusual. He told me that after the war, he'd joined the Communist Party and was still a 'Black Sea card carrying member'. He'd been on the freezing Navy ships, during the war, running supplies through to Murmansk, in the convoys. I never found out what Nobby was doing his time for, but he must've been in for something quite serious. Doug was a psychopath from up North in Yorkshire. I'd listen to him talk about killing people, how it was the right thing to do, if someone's insulted you, man. I made a mental note never to do anything that may be construed as an insult. Doug liked to talk, and I was a good listener, but some of the things I heard from him were extremely disturbing. He was obsessed with the occult. The screws on C-wing, unlike the rest of the prison, were not allowed to carry truncheons in their pockets. It was thought that the sight of sticks might get the patients restless.

The Topping Shed hadn't been used for a long time, but it still sent a shiver down the spine to stand in it. It was located near the end of the wing, and was kept unlocked, so I was using it to store some mopbuckets and brushes. Looking up the shute you could see the trapdoors, now nailed shut, and at the bottom there were stone brackets to hold the stretcher in place. It was easily the coldest room in the prison, and it didn't do to linger there.

C-wing was the oldest of the Parkhurst wings. It had clearly been built to house women and children; all the cell doorways were less than five feet six inches high. In its heyday, Parkhurst was a holding prison, before its inmates were deported to Australia. The prison-ship would anchor in the River Medina, and the convicts would be taken there, by way of a tunnel connecting the river with the prison. The tunnel is still said to exist although the ends have been long blocked-up to make the tunnel inaccessible.

Some of the C-wing men had been building their own tunnel; it was started under the shower house, and ran directly towards the outside wall, some 15 yards away. Unfortunately, quite by chance, a screw fell into it one day, so it had to be abandoned when it was only half finished.

The treatment hatch was open all hours to dispense the various drugs the men were on. Some of the cons saved their drugs up; they'd take their tot of Valium or Triptizol away back to their cells where they'd pour it into empty lemonade bottles. When a bottle was full it'd be sold for a half ounce of snout. Geezers were walking around on pink candyfloss most of the time. One of the men, the lifer called Keith, took an overdose one day and slipped into a coma. He was taken over to the hospital where an attempt was made to bring him round. The doctor told us that Keith could've been saved if he hadn't lost the will to live. He died. As I have said, I don't know what Keith had done, to be weighed off with a life sentence, but he never came over as a violent man—in all the time we knew him—but rather the opposite. Being involved in some way with the Salvation Army, his cell was neat and clean, and I guess we were too much of a nasty shock for him. The system had a way of sweeping suicides under the carpet, almost a denial that they ever happened. Keith's full name was Keith Hildersley. He was liked by all of us who knew him.

Colin began swallowing razor blades and bedsprings. He was taken out to the local casualty hospital where his stomach would be opened up and the metal removed. But no sooner was he brought back than he ate more bedsprings. It reached the stage where the doctors warned that they'd not be able to keep opening up the same wound every few weeks. Colin disappeared one day. The word had it that he'd been 'nutted off' to Broadmoor or Rampton.

Bill stuck his tongue out at me, to demonstrate the sort of drugs he was on. It was black. The Major spotted a dead rat one day. It was lying by the side of the workshop, and we had to pass it to get in through the door. The Major knelt down and tried to give the rat the kiss of life. We gathered round to watch, but the rat wasn't having any of it. A screw spotted what was going down, and he told the Major to stop it. The Major stood up, and, weaving around as was his way addressed the screw: 'Givvus a *wank* wi' the cheeks o' ya *bum*. Ugh!'

John had painted the inside of his cell black. When you went in there it was like falling into space. Nobby told me that he'd never get out of prison. His health was too poor, and he was an old man already. He'd die in prison. He knew this, and yet he still spent much of his time talking philosophy with anyone who'd listen.

'The system was devised by morons, to be administered by cretins . . . British Justice is a farce'.

I spent some time talking to Nobby about my arrest and the events leading from it. Nobby wasn't surprised at all.

'You're in need of a good solicitor, Alex—otherwise forget it. I can understand what you're saying, but there's a bloody awful lot of people to convince, and that's going to be very hard. You can do a rooftop, but the nick's so well concealed there'll be no one to see it. So, a waste of time that. D'you have many people outside to take up your case?'

'No'.
'It's important to stay in touch with the outside world. Let me think about it for a while, yeah?'

When a few days had gone by, he gave me an address.

'Drop a line to these people . . . they'll see you aren't messed about'.

It was the address of the Communist League.

'Would they know anything about my case?'
'Possibly, but I doubt it. You'd want the Communist Party for that. I guess the first thing is to write and let others know about you. The Communist League's different from the Party, they aren't so hard line, and the important thing is that they have two or three affiliated news-sheets, which reach more people than the *Morning Star*. They could give your case publicity. You're a political prisoner.

'This country doesn't have political prisoners, I've heard them saying that on the wireless'.
'That's to fool the public. If they're right, then you don't exist, and we're not having this conversation. Listen . . . I know about Special Branch and MI5; they operate against political targets. When an arrest is made they get the uniformed police to do it. But the people they nick are politicals right enough. They get sent to prison, and then cease to exist, because the government says there are no political prisoners. You're one of those people, Alex. I don't know what they've got in store for you, but I'd like you to promise never to let the bastards beat you. *Stay alive!* It is your *duty* to get through this, and let the people outside know you. Never forget this'.

'If I was fitted up, why was it Nobby?'
'The Branch couldn't nick you. That had to be done by the ordinary police. You couldn't be nicked for what they suspected you'd done, so you had to be nicked for something else. So lets suppose, as you say, they laid a burglary on you. That's all they could do if they wanted you inside regardless—and, if so, they got what they wanted. You're inside . . . and you don't exist. Very satisfactory'.

Woof. That was heavy!

'When were you sentenced Alex?'
'December seventy-one'

'Yeah. That fits'.
'What do you mean?'
'Well again, if what you suspect happened is correct, that was when they had a big scare on. Loads of Soviets, embassy officials, trade delegates sent packing. Tales of subversion and mayhem. A pound to a penny the counsellor you saw was one of them. Yeah, that was big all right. Serious. What interested the Branch was that you'd had direct contact with one of the main people, an embassy official. That, and because you lived in an area with a fairly substantial immigrant community, was what got them interested in you'.

'But, surely, someone can be found to verify what I'm saying? Other people must know the truth. So what have I to do to reach them?'
'You got to survive. That's the only way you're going to reach them'.

I thought that might be easier said than done.

• • •

One day, I heard that the Kray twins were being moved out of the special security block (SSB). The whisper was that they were coming onto C wing. And so they did.

Everyone was banged up one day after lunch, and when our doors were opened Ron and Reg had already moved in. Ron knocked on my cell door and introduced himself. He was my next door neighbour.

'Haven't you got a record player?', he asked.
'Nah. It's broken'.
'Right. Hang about a minute . . . '. He disappeared into his cell and came back with a large Dansette record player.
'You can use this for a while. You haven't any records have you?'

And he was gone again. When he returned he had a large pile of Tammy Yuro LPs.

'Use these for as long as you like. If I want them, I'll let you know'.
'Yeah'.

I was well surprised. The newspapers and the police said the twins were monsters of some sort. Mind you, I never did play anything on that Dansette; I wasn't going to scratch any records man . . .

• • •

My twenty-second birthday came and went without a party. Ha. One day, a black man came onto the wing. His name was Ervin, and he was in a pretty bad state. His self-confidence was practically non-existent, and he had great trouble finding other cons to talk to. He was obviously frightened and kept himself behind the door of his cell most of the time. He was the only black inmate on C-wing at that time, so there was no one that he could readily identify with. I spent some time with him, helping him to write letters home, to his parents and brothers and sisters. Ervin was illiterate.

After a few months the medics had him taken over to F2 for some sort of treatment programme. This meant he had to live over there, and he was quickly forgotten by the C-wing inmates. Then a month or two afterwards he was returned to us. By this time there'd been a couple of new men on the wing, and one of these was a National Front member, a white guy called John. This bloke couldn't abide blacks. It was a serious thing with him. Very heavy. One of John's first reactions to Ervin was to go to his cell and tell him to either tidy it up or get off the wing. John gave Ervin 30 minutes to do either. It was true; Ervin's cell was a bit of a mess, but not overly so. Most of the guys were on drugs, their motors running at reduced speed. During the daytime they'd go to the workshop to paint toy soldiers. In the evenings they'd watch TV until bang-up, then get into bed and fall asleep.

Thirty minutes came and went. John went back to Ervin's cell. I was in my own cell, unaware of what was going down. My cell door was open, and I remember I was writing a letter. Suddenly, I heard a scream, and the sound of someone running down the landing outside (the landings had wooden floors). I called out 'Oy! Can't you keep the fackin' noise down, I'm trying to write a fackin' letter . . . ?'

Then I saw Ervin dash past with a knife sticking in his back. John was chasing him, with the intention of pulling it out and giving it to him again. The screams alerted the screws, who came running up the stairs. Ervin changed his course, towards the screws, hoping naturally for their protection. Not so. The screws grabbed Ervin and wrestled him to the floor! Moreover, onto his back! The knife was driven further in. Some months later, I heard Ervin had won compensation and had been released, with only one lung to keep him breathing—his experience of prison clearly not making him a better person. The cons' opinion was that a lone black man should not have been located on a wing where there was another con who was a National Front member, and who was in prison for serious violence.

• • •

Nobby, the old-timer who had told me to *survive* and reach people, died. We never discovered how it happened. I remember Nobby as a man who was not intrinsically bad. He was unconventional and held contrary opinions. An old Communist, but an idealist. Violence was an anathema to him. Because of his views, views that didn't conform to the British standard, he found himself under the hammer. Once he told me that democracy was an illusion, a sham. There had to be a better way. His name was Nobby Clarke, a good friend and an enlightened man. RIP.

There wasn't a great deal of bang-up on C-wing—only at meal times and at night. We would collect our lunch at 11.30 a.m., and then be banged-up until 1.30 p.m. During the bang-up, there was only one screw left on the wing . . . the others would go for their own meals, and come back at around 1.25 p.m. If any of the men needed the toilet during the after lunch bang-up, they could ring their cell emergency bell and depending on who was left on duty be let out for a few minutes. This procedure was strictly unofficial. Some screws would allow it, but others wouldn't. One day, at around 12.30 p.m., the bell rang. Someone wanted the toilet. I heard the duty screw come upstairs and unlock one of the cell doors. Then I heard: 'Just make one wrong move and you're dead'.

I recognised the voice. It was one of the Northerners, a man called George. He was built big and not the kind to meet in a dark alley. Violent. There were the sounds of shuffling feet—George had got the screw round the throat and had a Stanley knife held there. They passed outside my cell and stopped at the next doorway.

'Get this fuckin' door opened!'

The geezer in the cell was my other neighbour, a Welshman called Gary. He was a touch older than I was—serving life. I hadn't thought he was the kind to get involved in serious trouble, but he could be easily led.

I heard the cell door unlock, and then, after a second or two, crash shut again. George and the screw were now locked in there with Gary. The time was around 12.35 p.m. Of course, the screw had been taken hostage. Within half an hour, the rest of the screws in the prison found out that their colleague had been taken. All of the usual activities— workshop, exercise, visits etc.—were shut down. All of the cons were told to go to their cells, where they were banged-up. The only people left on the landings were screws and associated prison staff. C wing began to fill up with screws. None of them had gone off duty. All had decided to wait until the end. Because I was next door, I could hear what was going down. George told the screws that if any of them tried to jack the door off the hostage would be killed. *Woof,* I thought. George you silly sod.

'We want a prison van, and a prisoner to drive it. We want to be able to travel to a field, where a helicopter can land. Then we want it to fly us to an airport . . . 'etc., etc.

Alice in Wonderland, in other words. I got up to stand on my table and look out of the window. A marksman with a rifle had arrived and was positioned across the way. So they were willing to kill, too. Naturally.

'Marksman outside fellas!', I called.

The 'situation' went on all day and into the evening. And all the time the screws were becoming increasingly restless, and more and more pissed off. We had to be fed at 4.30 p.m., but we were made to go and collect our meals singly. And then, surrounded by screws, a couple of hours later they allowed us a drink of diesel, each cell door being opened and closed one at a time. My door opened and Reg was there with a tea-bucket. Ron was with him. And half a dozen screws.

'Evenin' Alex. Drop of tea?'

Later on a police detective inspector turned up. Standing outside Gary's cell he tried to reason with them.

'Look', he said, 'I'm a policeman. I'm unarmed. Why don't you let the screw go—I'm willing to take his place . . . '
'Fuck *off!*"
'Who's the spokesman for you two? Is it you George?'
'I said fuck off! If you're deaf I can get you an extra ear. Do you want one? I'll cut it off this cunt . . . '
'No, no, no, George. Come on . . . be reasonable. Who's your mate? Gary is it? Take me instead, lads. I'm worth more than that poor bastard you've got there . . . '
'Where's our fuckin' helicopter?'.
'Don't worry George, you'll have it. But again, you'll be more successful if you've got me as a hostage instead of the officer in there. You haven't harmed him have you?'

After an hour or so the copper managed to convince George to let the screw go.

'Listen carefully, George. I have a pair of handcuffs with me. I'm going to fasten myself to the landing railing, so that when you let the officer go I'll be here for you, and you can take me in his place, OK? Now, don't panic. Another officer is going to unlock the cell door . . . as soon as he's done that he'll fuck off. When the door's open let Mr. L out of the cell slowly, and once he's clear, you can take me in his place . . . '

'How do we know you'll not do a runner as soon as we let him go . . . '
'George, haven't you been listening. I've handcuffed myself to the railing outside . . . *I can't* do a runner.'

I heard the screw go to unlock the door. Within a few seconds I heard Gary and George release the hostage. Then I heard the copper shout 'Move!'.

He'd not had the handcuffs closed, which meant he could slip them at any time. Both the hostage screw and the police inspector ran down the landing, away from Gary's cell.

In the meantime, George and Gary, taken by surprise, were left standing by themselves outside Gary's cell. At the same time I heard someone shout *'Chaaarge!'*, and the whole wing reverberated to the sound of fifty-odd screws' boots, as they sprinted towards the two cons. George had been carrying a Stanley knife and Gary a pair of scissors. As soon as they saw all the screws charging at them they both dropped their weapons and put their hands in the air. It didn't do them any good. The screws smashed into them and both cons were injured. The screams were animal screams. As a landing cleaner I was asked to mop the blood up afterwards. It quarter-filled a mop-bucket.

Both Gary and George were put down the block—and after being sentenced to another five years each they were both ghosted out. A few months later I heard that George was on hunger strike, up Strangeways gaol in Manchester. He died as he was being transferred to Gartree gaol. He'd been drugged-up and could only speak with difficulty.

Both George and Gary had been made desperate by the system. Their action was, for them, a shit-or-bust operation. They didn't harm the hostage, save for a slight nick above an ear. All they wanted was out . . .

CHAPTER SIX

One of my favourite programmes on the TV was a hospital drama series called 'Angels'. One day, I wrote to one of the actresses, F, and she wrote back. It was to be the beginning of a friendship that was to go on for many years. F was the first person I'd known who was human—that is since I'd come into Prisonworld. F was a lovely person, in so many ways, and I counted myself extremely fortunate to have her as a friend. Sometimes I'd write three times a week. I'd tell her anything. Sometimes when I was on a downer she'd help me to come out of it quicker than I would've done, and when she was depressed I would help her too. The screws didn't like me writing to her.

At that time there was no-one on the Out who wrote to me, except for my mother—and then only infrequently. I was one of the lifers who were 'alone'. The cons realised that the system was able to hurt you more if there were no people on the outside to kick up a fuss on your behalf if anything questionable was done to you by the screws. In a sense, you became more of a target. It was important, then, to forge some links on the other side of the wall.

F was a respectable woman, from an upper-echelon family. From the screws' point of view, it wouldn't pay for me to be too friendly with her. I found that my letters to her were sometimes stopped, and vice versa, by the prison censors.

• • •

I was still an A-Man, and this meant that everyone from the outside who contacted me would be security-vetted. One day, in a letter from my mother, she asked if I could get a photograph of myself taken so that she could see what I looked like. I applied to the governor for permission to have the photo taken, but he refused. So I petitioned the Home Secretary, who also refused. The reason I was given was that such a photo could be used for 'political purposes'. I wrote to my MP, Doug Hoyle, who took the issue up with the Home Office, and managed to get them to relent. The photograph was the same size as a passport photo, and it was in black and white. It looked exactly like a police 'mugshot'. It cost me four pounds to have it taken. In a photo booth on the Out, I would've paid half-a-crown for four such photos in colour. My weekly pay was such that I had to go without any pay at all for a fortnight to pay for the photo.

Permission for it had been given grudgingly, and they wanted me to suffer in consequence. It was typical of the system to concede something only to make you pay dearly for it in some other way later. With one hand it gave and with the other took away.

• • •

One day, I was walking around the exercise yard with my friend Chilly. Another con, Pete M came up to us, and started talking about one of the blokes on my landing, who was having a bit of trouble.

'He's getting out in a couple of months, so he's been saving his wages up to supplement his pension when he's released. Yesterday we found out that another con's been threatening to do him if he doesn't buy things for him in the prison canteen. It's been going on for a few weeks now, and the old guy's in tears . . . '
'Who's doing the threatening then?'
'That cunt in (cell) 48. We think that someone should have a word with him . . . '

The 'we' was significant. Pete M had a lot to do with Ron and Reg, and put himself about as their go-between and 'enforcer'. I thought he was a pile of shit but the twins seemed to trust him. The implication of the 'we' then, was Pete M and the twins. Also, the phrase 'have a word' meant 'use violence'.

'Hang about Pete', I said, 'what're you saying? You want me to go along to this guy's cell and have it out with him?' I was also thinking, if Pete M was so tough, why doesn't he do his own dirty work. He must've read my mind.
'I'd take care of it myself but it'd be too obvious. The screws are watchin' me all the fuckin' time'.
'Do Ron and Reg know about this?'. I wanted to be sure.
'What do *you* think . . . ?'
'I'll let you know before the end of the exercise, Pete. OK?'
'Don't take too long'.

Chilly'd heard it all, so I asked him what he thought.

'Doesn't sound right Alex. There's something wrong man. But I can't work out what . . . '
'If this does come from the twins it can't be refused'.
'I know'.
'Why not go and find out? See Reg'.

'Nah. If I did, it'd look as though I didn't trust M. That could have a bad return. I dunno to what extent he's in with the firm, but I don't want to be the one to find out . . .'

'So refuse it. Tell him the screws are watching you too'.

'Somehow I don't think that'd go down too well . . . who's the geezer in 48?'

'Mark. I don't know his surname. I don't have anythin' to do with him, but if the twins are involved . . .'

In the event I said 'Nothing personal, mate' and Chilly and I laid into him. We both went up in front of the Board of Visitors and were each awarded 56 days in solitary and we did the whole lot down in the block; it was no hardship, but I was pissed off that I'd have to miss the last couple of episodes of 'Angels'. As soon as the 56 days were served, we both went back to C wing. I went straight to my cell, to get my tobacco and roll a smoke. A few minutes later Pete M walked in.

'You', he began, 'are a bastard for doing that guy over . . .'

'What? Hang about, it was you who told us to do it!'

He punched me in the face. I kicked him in the balls.

'Right,' he said, 'I'm going downstairs to get a pair of scissors. When I get back up here I'm gonna plunge you!'

He left my cell on the run. Shit, I thought. I opened the cupboard and took out a sock then reached for a PP9 battery and slipped it into it. Then I waited. Fortunately Reg had heard the commotion and was out of his cell just as M was reaching the top of the stairs with the scissors. He told M to cool down and hand him the scissors, then, a few minutes later he looked round the door into my cell and told me to bang-up for a while until the situation was sorted.

The screws knew that something had gone off, but they didn't know what. I refused to tell them so they sent me over to F2. While I was over there I had plenty of time to think, and after a while, aided by a bit of feedback from some of the lads, I knew what had happened. M had wanted one of the cons beaten up, for personal reasons. But he didn't care to do it himself, so he approached Chilly and myself and told us porkies. The old guy who was getting out hadn't had liberties taken. The twins weren't involved. It was a scam. M had thought 'I want that guy beaten up. But I don't want to do it myself. I'll go to Alex and Chilly and give them the patter. If they do the business then both of them'll probably get ghosted which means my involvement will never be known. It'll look as though it was they who had the disagreement and it'll end there'.

But what M had certainly not counted on was our reappearance on the wing after the 56 days down the chokey . . . Further, he thought I was the only one who could implicate him—he'd not counted on Chilly; and Chilly was able to reach Reg to give him the full SP. When we were approached by M on the exercise yard, the element which didn't add-up was M doing this and not either Ron or Reg. If the twins wanted it they would've seen us themselves. I should've done what Chilly had suggested and gone to see Reg.

After a while over F2 I got the whisper that it was OK to go back on the wing, but I'd had enough of C-wing, and I asked to go on one of the main wings. The request was approved, and I moved my kit over to D wing. Pete M, incidentally was not serving a life sentence, he was released in the mid-eighties and went to live in the Midlands. He got a couple of impressionable youths together and told them he was a hard-man starting a firm up. To lend credence he showed the youths a photograph of the twins (he'd stolen it from Reg's cell) and told them he'd been given it by Reggie Kray. The youths were suitably impressed. Then apparently M asked for proof of their loyalty and commitment—they should each help to kill someone.

The three of them travelled to one of the National Parks in Cheshire and found some public toilets. They laid in wait until a guy showed up to use them. M and each of the youths attacked the man and buggered him and killed him. They repeated the same procedure a second time with another innocent man. But when they tried it a third time their victim grew suspicious and managed to leg it away. It was that man who raised the alarm. Anyway, M got a few life sentences and hopefully society'll never see him again. A few people want to 'have a word with him'.

● ● ●

Because my mom didn't travel well and because the Isle of White was too far away for her to reach easily (having to rely on public transport), I applied for permission to go to Strangeways on a temporary transfer so that I could have a few visits from her and also from my father. Permission was granted.

On the day I was taken to Parkhurst reception and put in a prison van, handcuffed to a screw. Two other screws sat in the back and there were two more, a driver and navigator up front. As soon as we left the gatehouse I saw flashing lights; it was a police motor waiting for us—

the jam sandwich took up position in front of the van and escorted us to the ferry.

It was Cowes Week. I could see all kinds of people milling about, arriving from Portsmouth for the event; I could see out of the special tinted windows, but no one could see in. There were not a few curious glances directed towards the van . . . it was a very curious thing, seeing people gazing directly at you, but only seeing dark glass. The van itself was painted a bright yellow, with the initials 'HMP' displayed above the front windshield. It was known as a 'Cat. A Van.'

Inside, a metal screen separated the back of the van from the driver and navigator, the latter having control of a powerful police radio which was left on constantly when the van was in use. The van was not allowed to stop. Rumour had it that a shooter was kept in a locked box under the rear seat. Should an A-man attempt an escape he would risk being shot and killed. As we rolled off the ferry at the Portsmouth end there were a further two jam sandwiches waiting. With lights flashing and sirens blaring the whole lot of us set off for Manchester.

As we passed through each county, the navigator would pick up the radio mike and enter a code word.

'Charlie One Category A transport approaching your net *en route* Manchester'.

As each county boundary approached, a fresh set of police cars would be waiting to take over from the last. The convoy made these changeovers without any reduction in speed. On the motorway the same operation followed—at 70 miles per hour and in the fast lane throughout.

It was 1976. The summer was long and unbearably hot and during the journey the inside of the A-van became like an oven. On the roads there were bottlenecks and contraflows but the police cars would forge ahead, their lights and sirens carving a path through, sometimes rudely forcing other vehicles into the verges. And all the while I'm sat there thinking and wondering how all that related to me . . . Before Parkhurst there'd never been police escorts. So what had happened to change that?

I'd close my eyes and focus back to 1971; to just before I'd been arrested. Then I'd been an ordinary kid, albeit a sometimes petty thief who stole while on the run. I had read some of Franz Kafka's stories but I'd never finish them because they upset me. It was almost as if I was the person he was describing. And then I'd think: 'But this is England. England—not a police state somewhere in Eastern Europe or Latin America. What's happening?'

I understood that—using all the security as a yardstick—I was not going to be free again, for a very long time. I had to reach someone—but who? My letters were all censored, and my visits closely monitored, and I knew that some of the letters I'd written had been stopped from being posted. Anything I wrote, if it was critical of my situation and, therefore of the system that held me, would be stopped from reaching its destination. I knew that. I was like a fly in a closed bottle. Eventually, I'd use up all the oxygen and die.

'The only way you're going to reach people Alex is to *survive*'.

● ● ●

Strangeways was wary of me. They put me down the block in a punishment cell, although I didn't have to put the bed out during the day, and I was allowed to use my radio. The visits with my parents (one at a time because my father and mother had split up) were spoiled . . . we could face each other over a table but on each of the other sides of the table sat two screws. I wasn't able to say anything confidential, neither were my parents, we were so conscious of the screws.

At nights, because Strangeways is classed as a local prison, the red light was kept on again, and my clothing had to be put in a cardboard box and left outside the cell as it was when I was at Walton gaol in Liverpool. Was it only four years ago? *Woof.* It seemed like an eternity. After a month at Strangeways I was back in a Cat. A van *en route* home to Parkhurst. When I got back I learned that there'd been an escape. The beauty of it was the escape had been executed from the SSB—the Special Security Block. The SSB was a prison within a prison, an ultra secure building housing only a dozen or so prisoners who presented the gravest threat to society. The building was surrounded by fences and razor wire, cameras and dog patrols. No one, it was thought, could burst out of there. But someone did.

Because of the heat of the summer some of the SSB cons were allowed to build a small lean-to against one of the fences. This was so that they had somewhere to sit down in the shade. The lean-to was a security blind spot . . . the cameras couldn't see inside it. C and a friend made for themselves a pair of wire-cutters; then, from inside the lean-to they cut a hole in the security fence and climbed through. This led them into the main prison grounds, which meant they had the prison perimeter fence to negotiate. Which they did! It was beautiful. There was also an eight foot-high concrete wall to get over. C climbed it and was over. His mate, unfortunately, was captured as he was climbing it.

It was done in broad daylight from under the noses of the screws. All of the cons that were on exercise that day watched it happen; it was a turbo boost for morale. C was recaptured on the third day in Parkhurst forest, after the whole of the Island's security forces, (including the army) had been mobilised for the search. But the blow had been struck. It had been demonstrated that, despite the endeavours of the Home Office to suppress, restrict and stifle humans, with heavy-handed security policies and devices, those same humans, given the will, could defeat and embarrass the lot of them when it came down to the question of intelligence and ingenuity.

I became friends with a mandatory Lifer called Von, otherwise known, rather fondly, as 'The Mad German'. Von was looking at a long long time in gaol, man. I guess we shared a common outlook, perhaps because we had parents who originated on the wrong side of the Berlin Wall. Von was scathing in his criticism of the British *status quo.*

'How can this fuckin' country call itself civilised Strog?' He called me "Stroganof", or "Strog" for short.
'I don't fucking know Von', I replied. He burst out laughing.
'No, seriously Strog . . .'
'Yeah, seriously Von . . .'. More laughter.

A curious practice at Parkhurst was allowing prisoners to have small plots of land to grow vegetables in. Von secured a plot and we both planted a strawberry patch. He also built a small greenhouse from bits of wood and sheets of plastic. Every couple of weeks the burglars would come and pull it down. Von just put it up again.

'They ain't gonna beat us Strog'.

The day came when the strawberries started to ripen. We slung a net over them to keep the birds off and then, one morning, we went down to the plot and found all the red ones had gone . . . Von put his head back and howled. He was well pissed off. This event happened to coincide with finding his greenhouse flattened yet again.

'It's the screws Strog. It's got to be'.
'Not necessarily. Could be cons making it look like it's the screws. Anyway if it is the screws they wouldn't admit to it'.

He pulled a chiv out of his pocket and tossed it in the air a couple of times. 'If I find out who it was . . . ' he threw the blade at a rotten piece of wood, piercing it with a dull thud.

For the next few days we put a few feelers out to see if anyone'd been enjoying strawberries and cream recently. But we never found the culprit or culprits.

• • •

In the next cell to mine was man who claimed to be innocent and who was serving 22 life sentences. When I thought of him I thought, 'And you think *you* got problems Alex . . . '

His name was Paul. He liked a drop to drink so every week I'd put two or three gallons of hooch down. These were always stashed under my bed, bubbling away in gallon containers with charcoal filters to cut the smell down. The screws all knew about it, I mean they couldn't mistake the smell. It was like a brewery. They didn't mind unless somebody got blind drunk and aggressive. Then they'd come down on everybody and confiscate all the booze. Paul and I would share the hooch between us. Sometimes I'd fill up a few vacuum flasks and distribute them around the wing. There was no charge. Nothing to pay. But I'd find I'd come back to my cell sometimes and discover parcels of tobacco or packets of biscuits left on the cot. Favours returned.

Prison hooch is underrated. If it's made properly it's not a bad drink—and cheap to produce. The best way is to get a plastic bucket and fill it three-quarters full with warm water. Rub into it an ounce and a half of bakers' yeast and pour in half a kilo of white sugar. Take a pound of unflavoured soya and throw that in too. Then keep the bucket covered with a loose lid and pour in a further quarter pound of sugar each day for five days. Then let the brew alone for another three days to allow the yeast to burn itself out. Finally, strain the lot into another container and it's ready for drinking. The first time I tried it I only had one pint and I was horizontal.

For a while I got involved with the horse racing. The bookie, Joe, would accept tobacco bets—a quarter ounce being the minimum—and cash bets without a limit. Every week I'd bet half an ounce. Another friend was a Hungarian called Laszlo. He was more of a compulsive gambler and, one day, inevitably, he got in over his head. He owed Joe a lot of snout and had no possible way of paying it off. More than this, he was in real danger of being paid a visit by Joe's heavies. I only had a half an ounce of snout in my name, which was nowhere near enough to pay Laszlo's debt. So I put it on a horse to win—and it did! The winnings went on another and that won, too. I had enough to give to Laszlo to pay his debt. That was the last time I made any bets on the horses and, to his credit, the last time Laszlo did too.

I was working in the tailor's shop for a while. It wasn't bad work and the money was reasonable. But I had to give up the job when the workshop was blown up. Parkhurst was full of 'characters'. Clive Duck and Dive did exactly that. I bought a few radios off him for tobacco. He had a wide selection of goods on offer. If it was illicit, he had it. Captain Bird's Eye was a mandatory lifer who'd murdered his wife and put her in the freezer. Crazy Horse was a mad black man who howled at the moon; often he'd hide in cell doorways and jump out in front of you, scaring you shitless. Von, my friend, like myself was an 'alternative' lifer. I had a long grey coat with a red star embroidered on one shoulder . . . I wore it every time I went out. Image is important in the dispersal's. Yeah, man.

Barney Rubble came up to me with a newspaper-wrapped parcel.

'Alex, I got somethin' to show you'.

He carefully unwrapped the parcel. Inside was a turd. It was bright green.

'Well? What do you reckon?'
'Where did it come from Barney . . . ?'
'From me . . . y'don't think I'd be carrying it around if it belonged to somebody else?'
'You got food poisoning, man. What you been eating?'
'Nothin' except the prison grub'.

By that evening half of the prison roll were down with food poisoning. Some thought it'd been done on purpose by the government. I never saw crap like that before. Still, it was ecologically sound.

One night the prison library was blown up. By chance I'd stayed awake that night, because I had a few letters to answer. At around half past one there was a tremendous explosion. I stood on my chair and looked out of the window; the night sky was filled with giant snowflakes fluttering down from a great height . . . they were pages from books, hundreds of them, thousands of pages. There was a ragged cheer from some of the other cons. The Fire Brigade was called in and I saw my first Irish Fire engine with the word 'EDAGIRB ERIF' beneath the radiator. The firemen climbed wearily out going, 'Shit, not Parkhurst again'.

• • •

A couple of cells away was a geezer, a lifer who was not a little overweight and tried to combat it by a run around the exercise area each day. He dropped down with a heart attack and died. I was given a job in the 'Light Textiles' shop working a sewing machine. The workshop produced curtains for the Prison Service and the MoD. It was staffed by civilian instructors. There were men working there who the politicians decreed were too dangerous to release. Psychopaths. Yet those same men were entrusted with enormous tailors' shears, sharp as anything, for cutting-up bolts of cloth. It was obvious that they weren't dangerous at all, there wasn't a single incident of a civilian (or a fellow con) being attacked. The observation was important. I realised the people outside were fed lies about prison and prisoners.

One of the classic lies is the one the public is always told whenever a prisoner escapes. It goes as follows:

'Do not approach this man. He is dangerous. If anyone should see him please contact the nearest policeman'.

The lie is told simply to reduce the chances of the escapee staying out. Most of the so-called violent men I've met present no risk to society. I was also learning about psychological violence. Von tried to interpret it in its simplest form,

'An old woman is crossing the street and a kid goes up to her and slaps her. She feels hurt. Alternatively, an old woman is crossing the street and a kid shouts abuse at her, calling her a silly old bag an' all that. She feels hurt. Both hurts are one hurt. Yes?'

I also learned that punishment is inflicted harm (otherwise it wouldn't be punishment). The question was 'How much inflicted harm is it safe to inflict without the process becoming torture . . .?

CHAPTER SEVEN

I was becoming criminalised. Prison is another world, a darkened society. If environment does determine consciousness—and I believe that it does—the prison environment induces a darkened consciousness. Everybody agrees that prison is an abnormal environment. Therefore, reactions to it must be in kind. To accept prison life fully is to accept the abnormality and become a part of it.

The public is often presented with the ins and outs of prisoners' protests, the tabloids point to 'trouble-makers' and scream for more suppressive powers to shut them up. Everyone, it seems, misses the central point that if prisoners are subjected to an abnormal environment, they too, after a while, become abnormal. It is possible to fight against it, but to do so means taking on the Home Office and refusing to comply with its dictates. After a while on A-wing, I was moved back onto C-wing. There were a couple of new faces I hadn't seen before, but everyone else I knew.

● ● ●

Late one afternoon there were half a dozen of us in the TV room watching a Rolf Harris programme. Halfway through it, the door opened and Doug walked in. He pulled the plug from the mains socket and went over to the television and switched it off, then with slow deliberation he picked up the TV set and threw it across the room where it exploded like a bomb, showering the room with slivers of glass. This done, Doug went off to play table tennis. The geezers who'd been watching the TV were still sat there as though nothing had happened. They were still watching Rolf Harris although there was no telly there anymore . . . Super had Doug removed to F2 landing for 'treatment'. Most of the guys heaved a sigh of relief—everyone knew that Doug was operating on a short rein and that his flight deck was fucked. None of us wanted to be around when he kicked off. Incredibly, Doug was sent back to the wing a few days later!

Just before bang-up one evening, I was on my way down the landing to look in on Doug and give him a few roll-ups—we all knew that he'd not got any smokes—but on the way I was asked into Stuart's cell for a cup of diesel and a chat. A couple of other cons were in there. Stuart wasn't a lifer. I don't know what he was doing time for, I think he was one of those unfortunate people who was supposed to be in a psychiatric hospital or something. He was around 30 years old, but had a mental age of 16 or 17.

'Hello Alex', he said. 'Come in and sit down, fancy a cup of tea?'
'Has it got sugar in it?'
'Ah, come in and shut up'.

Sugar is a rationed commodity in prison. Each inmate usually gets a small bag of it each week, but it doesn't stretch very far. I sat down and rolled a smoke, lit it, and had a few swigs of diesel.

'What's happening then fellers?'
'Stuart says it's possible to travel back in time', Andy told me.
'I wouldn't mind travelling back in time Stu, to before I had this lot laid on me . . . !'

Stuart wagged a finger. 'I'm not b-b-being taken seriously'. He had a bad stutter. 'I'll g-g-give you the scientific evidence tomorrow'.

Bob, the other guy in the cell, got up to go.

'I'm off down the happy hatch to pick me treatment up'.
'Bob do me a favour? Drop these cigs off at Doug's, he ain't got any smokes'.
'OK Alex. You got one for me?'
'Take one from the ones I just gave you for Doug'.
'Cheers. Good night everybody'.
'Night Bob'.

Stuart asked me if I still wanted to sell my budgie. It was a beautiful white and blue cock aged eleven months. He cost me an ounce of snout with the cage thrown in a few months earlier when I was on A wing. I'd been teaching it to talk and it had a few words, especially when I turned the cell light out at night. I'd never locked him in his cage. I just wasn't able to do that.

'I might do Stuart, if it's going to a good home. Trouble is he likes to eat pictures on the wallboard and he craps everywhere. Other than that, well, he's very well behaved'.
'How much?'
'The same as I paid for him, an ounce of snout . . .'
'Do I get the cage as well?'
'Yeah, man. With two packets of Trill, five sheets of sandpaper and three millet sprays . . . !'

At that moment the door opened and Bob walked back in. He looked an odd shade of grey and he was puffing nervously on his roll-up, his hands shaking all the while.

'Alex, Doug's door was locked so I couldn't give him the fags . . . I er I looked through the spyhole and there's somebody in Doug's cell with him . . .'
'Steady on, geez. What d'you mean there's somebody else in there with him? Who?'
'I don't know. Whoever it is I think he's dead'.
'Eh?'
'Shit—it looks fuckin awful'. He dropped his cig on the floor and bent down to pick it up.
'Sit down Bob. Move up Andy. I'm off down Doug's cell to see what the fuck this is all about'.

Doug had his cell just a few doors down the landing. When I got there the door, just as Bob had said, was banged-up. I looked through the spyhole and saw Doug sat in front of his table with his head on his arms as though he'd fallen asleep. Then I saw, on the cot, one of the other lifers, a guy called Brian who was doing time for killing his lover, a male nurse I think. I knew it was Brian, although his face was going black with odd splotches of purple covering it. He looked as if he'd been stabbed and garrotted. Murdered.
    I heard the screw shout for bang-up, unaware of the situation in Doug's cell. When he did find out the screw went apeshit. 'Get behind your doors NOW!', he yelled. 'Bang-up, Bang-up, NOW!' Five minutes later the wing was quiet although guys were shouting out of their windows trying to find if anyone knew what was going down. Half an hour later a medical screw came round each cell dishing out doses of tranquillisers and sleepers. An hour later everyone was knocked out. In the early hours of the morning I was woken-up by a screw shaking me awake; behind him there were two civvies with notebooks out looking at me through squinty eyes.

'Wake up! These two gentlemen would like to ask you a few questions. Are you awake?'

I was severely drugged-out from the tots of medication I'd had a few hours earlier. Focusing was difficult. One of the civvies said

'We're police officers investigating the murder of Brian Peake. What can you tell us about your movements last night . . . ?'

'Well I didn't go down the pub, I remember that'.
'Very funny. Ha. The quicker we get this over with the quicker you can get back to sleep'.

Fortunately I had an alibi of the best kind. For most of the evening I'd been working in the pantry. Then I'd done a few rounds of toast. A screw had been with me throughout.

'We'll be asking the officer what he has to say'.
'Good night'.

Next morning I found that some of the other cons had been similarly visited in the night. Later still, we discovered that Doug had received a bad letter and had simply decided to kill the first person that came into his cell. I couldn't help wondering what might have happened if I'd gone to his cell earlier in the evening with the cigs I had for him . . . Doug was a big lad. Strong. I may well have taken Brian's place.

• • •

It was a few weeks later and I was back over in the main prison, this time on B-wing. I'd made friends with another lifer called Tony and we were both together drinking diesel and having a smoke.

'Doug shouldn't've been allowed back on the wing after the incident with the television set', Tony was saying. 'It was fuckin' obvious the guy was freakin' out. Moving him back was a mistake, man'.

I told him I agreed. It was obvious that someone'd slipped-up.

'It seems they can get away with fackin' anything!'
'But what can we do about it, Tone? Nobody'll listen to us; we're cons, man. Dog shit on the pavement. I'm innocent and nobody'll listen to me. We ain't people, man, we're lifers'.
'We need some sort of platform. To teach people'.
'That can only be done through the media, they're the ones who can present it'.
'You still got that sample?'
'Sure'.

The sample was a tot of 'medication' of the sort dished out on C wing. The thing was, we didn't know what the stuff was. It wasn't Triptizol or Largactil or Valium or Mogadon. The drug was of a type that, when taken, produced strange side effects; it made you want to sit down, then stand up and then sit down and stand up; it induced a deep restlessness. We were pretty sure that it was an experimental compound that was being tested on prisoners before being put onto the open market.

The only drug I knew of which came close to producing similar effects was Amanazin. This was a controversial compound being used in the Soviet Union by Dr Daniel Luntz, a KGB colonel who ran the Serbski Institute for Forensic Psychiatry in Moscow. The West had been up in arms over it.

'It doesn't matter if it's Amanazin or not, Alex. It's dodgy stuff. What matters is that we got to find out what it is, and that means having somebody analyse it for us. We'll have to find a chemist or a pharmaceutical laboratory somewhere . . . it's a problem'.
'Suppose I took it to the Board of Visitors? They're meant to be independent . . . what do you think?'
'If you do that you'll have to declare your intent to the screws because they'll be in the room when you see the BoV. I don't think it'd be a good idea to show our hand before we're ready. There again, we don't have a connection to an outside chemist or anything . . . it's a difficult one, this'.
'It could be smuggled out the back door, I suppose. Risky, though'.

In the end I decided to take it to the BoV. I made an application to see them and an appointment was fixed for a day later in the week. The screw had asked me what I wanted to see them about; obviously I couldn't tell him the truth or I'd be in real trouble, so I said it was personal. When the day came I collected the drug sample and waited for the call-up. In the event it was a single member of the BoV I saw, a woman called Heather F. I had to stand in front of the desk she was sat at. Behind me at each shoulder stood the two screws.

'Mr Alexandrowicz? What can I do for you?'

I put my hand in my pocket and withdrew the drug sample. I felt the two screws stiffen behind me.

'I'd like you to take charge of this. It's a sample of one of the drugs being given out on C-wing and I have very good reason to believe it is experimental. Will you have it analysed?'

She sat further back from the desk as though to distance herself from the small bottle I put in front of her.

'Shit', I thought, 'she doesn't want to know'.

'A man was murdered recently over on C-wing. The man responsible was being given similar drugs . . .'—the inference being, of course, that the effect of the drugs was in a direct way connected. The woman looked frightened.

'I only want the Board of Visitors to take this sample and have it analysed', I told her. 'If the stuff turns out to be harmless, no problem. This is what I want to find out. Will you help?'

She looked behind me, obviously at one of the screws. Then she said there was nothing she could do until she'd consulted a quorum of members of the BoV.

'That won't take long. A couple of days. Why don't you keep hold of it and wait 'til I get back to you'.

'Well it isn't as simple as that. The first thing these two are going to do', I was referring to the screws behind me, 'when I leave this office is take the sample away from me. I'd really prefer that you took it with you'.

One of the screws spoke up. 'I think he's being a little paranoid Ma'am'.

'I agree. Keep hold of the phial and we'll meet again in two days'.

Dismissed, I left the office and headed back to my cell. A minute later the cell door burst open and half a dozen screws piled in. I was given a strip-search. The phial was taken off me. The screws, burglars, searched every inch of my cell—even inside my correspondence and between the pages of books! They took the cell furniture apart and pulled photographs from the wallboard, tearing them in the process. My radio was dismantled and 'accidentally' dropped on the floor.

• • •

Later that evening Tony came to my cell and I told him what'd happened.

'Well that's no surprise Al. The thing is you're gonna be watched more closely from now on'.

'Yeah, but that was an attempt to do the business legally. To let the BoV know and get them to handle it. No one can say now that we haven't tried to utilise legitimate channels. OK, so now we put it out through the back door'.

'We have to find someone to do that. Is there a bent screw we could use?'

'Not that I know of. Anyway I wouldn't trust it to a screw, bent or not. I know a geezer over on D wing, Tony, he's due a visit from his brief next week; I could ask him to slip it over that way. Where would we send it, though? Have you any contacts to get it to?"

'How about the *Daily Mirror*?"

'That sounds feasible. We're agreed then?'

'Agreed'.

'By the way, I want you to meet a couple of geezers who've just got back from Rampton. They've got stories to tell. About the treatment there. Horror stories, Alex. They should be written down and smuggled out too'.

'If we're going to get really involved we'll need to get a team together. How does this sound; we do the unthinkable and get a human rights group started . . . ?'

'With just prisoners as members?'

'Hmm'.

'I dunno. We'd have to build up credibility. No one ever listens to cons. Everything we do would have to be straight. No lies, no supposition. Facts. The idea sounds good. It's never been done before'.

'So let's do it'.

'Have you thought it through?'

'Yes. In theory anybody can start up a human rights group. Anyway, there's no reason why prisoners themselves can't do it. No reason why we can't. In fact I'd say prison's the logical place to have a group working, there's so much Official Secrets shit covering the gaols. But that don't apply to us. Get a few of the lads together an' we'll have a meeting tomorrow sometime'.

The group was to become the LHRO—The League for Human Rights Observance.

CHAPTER EIGHT

One of the people I came to know fairly well was another lifer called Steve. Steve was, like myself, a *discretionary* lifer, one who hadn't committed a capital crime. He was serving his sentence for GBH. Steve was a big man in every respect, in size, thought and in his concern for others. Also, in his actions.

One day we were walking around the exercise compound, talking about prison politics, of our perception of the current policies from the Home Office, and about life in general. After a while we shut up and carried on in a companionable silence.

'Alex. Let's go on the roof'.
'Sounds OK, When?'
'Now'.
'OK'.

The roof we singled out wasn't one of the wing roofs but a smaller one on top of one of the workshops. There was no specific reason for going up there. It wasn't in protest about the food, or the working conditions or the rates of pay. It wasn't political. To the people outside, it would have been interpreted as an act of mindlessness, done by bolshie prisoners. So why did I agree so readily? Steve and I raced for the building and began climbing the wall, before any of the screws knew what was happening. Half the prison was out there walking around, and there was a loud cheer when the guys saw us haring up the drainpipe. The screws saw what was happening and immediately stopped the exercise. All the cons were told to go back to the wings. Ten minutes after we reached the roof the whole of the compound had been cleared. The silence was beautiful.

'They might try rushing us', Steve warned. If the screws thought they could get us down quickly by bringing ladders and grabbing us bodily, they would. 'We got to prevent that'.

He disappeared over an adjoining roof and came back with a lump of timber. The Corned Beef[1] came out first and initiated the ploy to get us down.

---

[1] The chief officer. The most senior-ranking of the officer grades. This rank was abolished in 1987.

'Now, fellers. What the fuck you up to? Steve. Alex?'

He was looking at Steve and calling him Alex! Obviously he'd done a quick job finding out our Christian names, but he had to guess to find out which of us was which!

'Afternoon chief. We're just stayin' out here for a while', Steve responded. 'We don't want any trouble. This is a peaceful demo'. He had the lump of wood in one hand tapping it against his knee. 'So piss off and leave us alone'.
'So what about you, Steve? the chief asked addressing me. 'This isn't like you at all . . . '
'We ain't coming down', I said. 'End of . . . '

After a while a few screws came out and brought a sentry box, which they set up a few yards from the bottom of the building. A brazier was also put in place and lit by one of the screws.

'They're settling down for a wait, Steve'.
'Maybe. Could be that's what they want us to think'.
'Yeah'.

After a while the screw in the sentry box was left on his own. The air was getting a little parky and he was huddled over his brazier to keep warm, rubbing his hands and turning up his tunic collar. He called up to us:

'Alright fellers?'
'Yeah, mate', I answered. 'How's yourself?'
'Can't complain'.

He was something like 20 feet below us but the air was so still and crisp that we didn't have to shout.

'You look like a scene from *Hard Times*'. Steve told him.
'Feel like one'.
'I bet you don't do so bad on your bloody wage, mind'.
'I know, lad . . . An' I've managed to wangle triple-time for bein' out here . . . '

Silence.

'You mean you *want* us to stay up here . . . ?'
'Aye, lad'.

Steve looked over to me. 'Fuckin' system', he spat.

The exercise compound was an area comprising three workshops, two redgrass areas and a sloping football field. The compound was segregated from the prison wings by high walls. Access was given by a door of normal size, otherwise kept double-locked, set into one such wall. It was a couple of hundred yards or so away from the workshop roof but easily within sight, so that as soon as the door opened we could see it was the deputy governor coming through.

'Shit. We got royalty'.

We watched as the dep crossed the football field towards us. I knew him to be a fair and tolerant man. Experienced. Of course he'd have to be, to be placed in control of Parkhurst, man. I'd never seen a governor walk across a football field before. There was a sense of normality generated, a flashback to an earlier time, a time which became physical as it coalesced around me for a lingering moment . . . the last memory of being so alone with so few people on a football pitch was 1961, when I was a child of eight. I was taking a short cut to the newspaper shop to buy the latest issue of the *Dandy*. Corky the Cat was on the front cover painting the numerals 1961 on the fence making great play of the way the date read the same upside down. So the date was the first week of January 1961. Freedom had reached out and jolted me to remind me that it hadn't got around to saying goodbye yet and I better not forget it. It was the most wondrous thing, the beauty of if. The dep was unaware of the high art of the spell he had cast.

'You're both going to catch 'flu up there', was the first thing he said when he'd got close enough.
'We're OK', Steve replied.
'It's going to be dark soon. A bitter night tonight, according to the forecast . . . come on down and let's get a hot drink in you'.

The screw in the sentry box had come out, and was standing just behind the governor. He was rolling his eyes and shaking his head at us.

'Nah. I think we're alright where we are'.
'Well. It's your funeral. What's the point of this anyway? Is there a reason for this?
'Why not come up here and you may see things from our point of view. Alex, make way for the governor . . .'

For a moment I thought he was going to take up the offer. I guess the thought went through his head, but it went clean out the other side.

'The chief got your names mixed up. I don't think he'll be back out here again tonight. Embarrassed. Anyway . . . when you want to come down just say so and I'll be back'. And, on that note, he took his leave. He was right about one thing. It was beginning to come down dark and the temperature dropped and kept going. The usual season for rooftops was in the summer, when it was warm and balmy—the Funny Season. But early November was leaving it a bit late. Steve called down to the screw in the box.

'Hey mate. We did you a favour there. How about you doin' us one . . . you got a drop of spirits in your tea flask?'

The words came out with clouds of breath behind them. The screw said he hadn't though he said he'd test it to find out and poured himself a mug of hot tea. Over the compound wall we could see the upper storeys of B wing. The cell lights were on, so it must've turned half past eight. I was sat huddled up in my grey coat. It went down to my ankles, but the cloth was cheap prison material and let in the cold—I was beginning to freeze! Steve was built of sturdier stuff. But just before midnight he could see that I was in trouble.

'Alex. You OK, man?'
'Sure'.
'You're goin' down with pneumonia, man. Let's call it off, then. We've done what we wanted and got our bit of fresh air. Besides, we're payin' that cunt down there for as long as we stay up here. Can you get down the drainpipe?'
'I think so, Steve'.

We were taken straight down the block and the next day we were weighed-off by the deputy governor. We both got three days block and spent the whole of it asleep. So what about my reasons for going on the roof? I guess it was the prospect of not being banged-up in the cell for a while, I'd forgotten what it was like to stay out in the open air for any length of time. It was the first time I'd ever seen the stars—the sky was full of them. It was difficult to see the stars from behind a cell window; the prison's outside lighting system cast an orange glow over the premises, which was very hard to see through. The silence also was beautiful because there is never any on the wings. Although I caught 'flu I valued the experience, it was harmless to the rest if the prison and caused no trouble. It really had been to get a breath of fresh air and a whiff of freedom, no more than that.

• • •

A sailor can stay at sea for a very long time but it becomes vital to step foot on dry land every now and again . . . Of course, the Home Office would make sure we paid for the inch of freedom we'd stolen; over and above the three days punishment we'd been given down the block, I was on Mogadon to get me to sleep at nights. When I was first prescribed it, it was meant to ease the effects of earache—I'd gone to the doc to ask for something to ease the pain and he asked me if I was sleeping all right. I told him that I usually changed sleeping positions during the night, lying on my right side for a while, then on my left, then back to my right side. It was my right ear giving me gyp, especially when I turned over onto it. So a doctor prescribed me a sleeper, Mogadon. After a week I was called up again.

'Do you still have the earache? I'm prescribing another course of antibiotics for you. Are you finding it easier to sleep?'
'Like a log with the Mogadon'.
'Good. Well, I think we'll keep you on it for another week and then review the situation. Your earache should be cleared up by then'.

Of course nobody was ever told that Mogadon was addictive—I'd never known about it. But at the end of the second week I decided not to go back to the doctor to ask for more. Then, of course, I found that without the sleeper I was laying awake all night. After three days of staying awake I couldn't stand it no more and I had to go back to the doc to ask to be rewritten-up for the Mogadon. I wasn't cautioned about it or anything. It was simply re-prescribed. My earache had long gone.

The use of addictive drugs was a commonplace practice, and they seemed to be given regardless of whether or not people needed them. The reason for this was simple. Prisoners became more docile and less outspoken, and they could be threatened with removal of the drugs if they didn't do what they were told. Spending an extended time locked in a box was not a pleasant experience, nor was it ever meant to be— understandably, but to a prisoner it was made much worse if he had to spend sleepless nights as well. There are 24 hours in a day. If one could sleep for eight hours, the day was reduced to 16 hours. With the aid of drugs one could sleep ten hours, thus reducing the day further.

Sleep is the most prized commodity in prison. In reality, the prescribing of drugs had a contrary effect to the design woven by the authorities. In most cases, although prisoners did appear docile and more pliable, they simply went underground and expressed their anger more secretively. One day, it was announced that all drugs would be dispensed in the evenings, from each of the wings, instead of from the central dispensary. This was supposedly to improve efficiency.

Hitherto all dispensing was done from just the one room, which meant it was used by all the men in the prison, and long queues took a fair bit of time to deal with. So it was considered a better procedure if all the wings had their own dispensary. In practice all it meant was that the medic screws brought over each wing's treatments and the men picked them up from the SO's office before being banged up for the night. My sleeper, Mogadon 15mg, was left with the rest of the men's treatments on a shelf in the B wing SO's office.

After a couple of days I went to pick my drug up as usual. A line of medicine tots waited, each one with the name of the man for whom it was meant. I asked for mine—was given it—and took it back to my cell as usual. But when I tasted it I discovered that it wasn't Mogadon. I hadn't been banged up yet and I asked the man in the next cell to me, Noel, to taste a minute drop in the hope he'd know what it was. But he didn't. (Noel was a Provisional Sinn Fein Volunteer and wasn't on any of the drugs). He said it'd be best if I waited until next morning and pulled the doctor who had to walk past my cell every day to go to the treatment room between B and C-wings. As an idea it was a good one— so I decided to wait as Noel had suggested.

First thing next day I went to see a friend who may have been able to tell me what the drug was. He said he recognised it as a particularly high dose of Tunyl but he wanted to check it out with somebody who was on the stuff, so he got a second opinion. He was right the first time. Tunyl. Very high dosage. I went back to my cell and ate my breakfast, a chippolata sausage and half a tomato with a mug of diesel and a round of nick bread. Noel dropped in from next door and the two of us waited for the doctor to make his appearance. The word had been passed around the landing and most of the men were waiting with us. Within a few minutes the doctor appeared. I stood outside my cell with the tot of Tunyl in my hand and made to address him as he walked past but he wasn't having any of it.

'You make an appointment to see me. I'll talk with you tomorrow . . .'.
'Doctor, I believe there is something wrong with my treatment and I want to know why this was left for me last night . . .'.

Out of the cell doorways the other cons appeared and began to surround the doctor. He began to look about him and started to panic.

'Now—calm yourself down now', Noel told him. 'All we want you to do is tell this man', indicating myself, 'why he was given such a high dose of Tunyl when he should only have been given Mogadon. Now, you tell him, doctor, otherwise there could well be trouble over this'.

The doctor wasn't daft. 'Very well. I don't know why he was . . .'.
'Why don't you face him when you talk to him'.
'Yes. I don't know why you were given this medication, I certainly didn't prescribe it. There seems to have been a mistake. I will make an investigation'.
'That sounds reasonable Noel'.
'Well doc, don't take too long with your investigation will you? Alright fellers, let the man pass'.

For the next couple of months, I made a series of applications to see a doctor, to ask for the result of his 'investigation', but each time I was fobbed-off until he made it pretty clear that he hadn't done anything at all and that I was wasting my time. In the end I was made to feel guilty for bothering the doctors, so I gave up on it.

• • •

I guess I was a rebellious prisoner in those days. I was very much my own man, and I wouldn't play the Home Office games. As far as I was concerned I was innocent of the crimes I was imprisoned for. I knew one day the truth would come out, but that it needed outside investigation to prove the strength of what I was saying. In the meantime I wouldn't be treated as a guilty felon. I was in prison because, to my mind, I was stitched up by the police and I was not going to lie down and pretend the Home Office's treatment of me was just. For it was not.

Noel, my next door neighbour on B wing was in prison because of his activity as an IRA bomber. When I first met members of the Provos I was surprised. Surprised because the media had portrayed them as mindless thugs and wanton psychopaths, as villains of the very worst kind. And yet . . .

Noel was a young man in his twenties, yet despite his youth, he was cultured with a refined sense of morality. 'Oh, sure', I can hear people say. But it's the truth. There was a firm gentleness in Noel, and an air of nobility about him and his actions. I tried hard to understand his philosophy and—perhaps because I'd given so much thought to it—I became increasingly more understanding. Beginning with the hypothesis that England had been invaded by the Irish and that the Irish had taken for themselves Liverpool, Manchester and towns in

between and refused to leave, claiming that they had a right to hold on
to that land as their own for whatever reason they might have, and
partition it from the rest of England, and raise the Irish tricolour over
the Liver building, and then persecute the (former) English residents of
that partitioned state, my guess is that the English would be pretty
severely pissed off. Perhaps to the extent of forming small bands of men
and women to conduct a campaign of harassment and armed response.
Would the English in the partitioned state begin a resistance movement
to oust the Irish 'aliens'?

The likelihood is that they would. The Irish would call them
'terrorists'. Criminals. To the rest of the English they would certainly
be perceived as freedom fighters. Someone once said that the English
sickness is hypocrisy and that ain't too far short of it, man.

'What about targeting civilians, women and children?'
'Remember how the present troubles began Alex. Bloody Sunday, yes? A
peaceful march made up of just such civilians, men, women and kids
alright? The bloody Brits fired live rounds into them, a slaughter Alex.
We don't target women and children. That's a Brit lie. That's the
misinformation put about by the Tory newssheets. We have to fight a
dirty war. There's no way we can mass our forces, armed with AK47s
and armourlite, a few drainpipe mortars and a light machine-gun
captured in Armagh, against a British army massed wheel to wheel
with Chieftain tanks and armoured vehicles, rocket launchers and
missile-carrying helicopters and gunships. Does that make sense? We
try to get our men militarily trained so we don't have idiots behind our
triggers, so that the risk to civilians is cut down. But every so often we
have to use volunteers who haven't had proper training and it's true
that rounds have gone astray or an explosive device hasn't detonated
at the right time . . . We are conducting a guerrilla war, no mistake, and
to win it we have to keep the sympathy and support of the civilian
population. How in God's name are we supposed to do that if we get
together and say "Right, let's target innocent civilians?". We aren't
the ones responsible for Nagasaki and Hiroshima; nor Dresden and
Cologne. We are not the ones who napalmed whole villages in Vietnam
and Laos. Of all the guerrilla wars going on around the globe we have
caused less civilian casualties . . . We want our country back'.

I rolled a cigarette.

'Alex the ordinary people on the street, they know the situation in
Northern Ireland is wrong. They want the troops out just as much as we
do . . . They fear for a bloodbath . . . No. That's the misinformation

again. They said exactly the same thing when the Brits withdrew from Eire more than 50 years ago. There was no bloodbath'.

• • •

I was in correspondence with the Communist League, taking their courses and learning about socio-economic problems and theories. I was a candidate for the Southampton cell and no doubt would have become a full member but I was warned that the Home Office took a dim view of me associating with such people and so I stopped the correspondence. Also I was writing fairly regularly to a friend who worked for Radio Moscow, Irina Proklova, and I was told to tie up that contact also. The reason for me being interested in Socialism stems from the fact that I had family living in Eastern Europe and I wanted to understand the system they had to live under. Another reason was that I was ignorant of Communism, and I wanted to know more so that I could discuss the ins and outs of it with better authority. I could go into any art gallery and admire a work hung on the wall, but I couldn't talk about it because I knew practically nothing of different schools of art and the techniques of individual masters. It was necessary, then, to learn about the theory so that I knew more and would be able to hold my own in any in-depth discussion. My approach to Communism was identical. I was tired of people slagging it off who weren't able to explain why. Who knew nothing but pretended to know everything.

'It's a free country, Alex, you ought to be able to write to who you like', Chilly told me. 'Shit, they got your body man, and they want your mind as well? Shit'.

But that was the way of it. The authorities must have been paranoid because of what I was in for. They probably still believed that the Embassy counsellor had given me information and that I was still up to something; maybe I was corresponding with Communists to bedevil the people who had taken away my life and put me in a box. There may have been some truth in that. Not that it mattered. As Chilly said, they'd got my body but they would never, ever, take control of my mind.

'Alex', Tony said to me one day as we were talking over policy for the LHRO, 'be careful. You're becoming an apologist for the bloody Provo's, man. They'll crucify you at the Home Office when they find out . . . '
'Screw the Home Office. I ain't got anything to thank the Home Office for. They're worse than anyone in this nick. Shit, so they got Crown immunity, so they can't be prosecuted. It's a good fucking job or there'd

be no politicians left. OK. So I ain't an apologist for anyone, man. Maybe I can see what's wrong. There's sod all I can do about it, but maybe I'll write about it one day. These politicians, man, they got some accounting to do one of these days, they won't keep on getting away with it forever. One day the world's going to see that the sun don't shine out of English arses'.

'Try being less outspoken, that's all'.
'Why? Don't tell me this ain't a free country after all. Don't tell me I'll be punished for speaking the truth, or speaking what I see to be the truth . . . For refusing to believe the politicians!'
'It isn't like you to be as bitter as this'.
'Well I guess I got just cause'.
'Nor as subjective'.
'You know . . . a country like this . . . it's being destroyed by its own leaders Tony. It is. Who would disagree with this? You?'
'There's nothing the likes of you or me can do about it . . . '.

'That's everybody's excuse. Look at the people out there. They get up in the morning and go to work. When they finish work they come home, eat a meal and either switch off in front of the telly or go down the pub and get pissed; go home, go to bed and wake up the next morning and repeat the whole process. They pick up a newspaper and give it a glance through before getting to the really interesting bits; the telly page and what the stars say . . . they ain't programmed to question what's being done on their own behalf. They don't want to know shit. They ain't concerned. Not, that is, until they get fitted up or until they're told their children can't have proper medical treatment because the bloody hospitals aren't funded properly . . . *then* they become concerned and they find they can't do owt about it because nobody else is so concerned. *Woof*.

'That's not true of everybody'.
'No it isn't. There are people who have everything they want. The bosses and controllers, civil servants, aristocracy, politicians. They're the ones who make the laws designed to protect themselves from the common rabble, not for the good of the people mind, but for the good of themselves'.

Tony had been sitting at his small cell table, putting the finishing touches to a jewellery box he'd made. When the lid was raised, it played *The Impossible Dream*. Inside it had been lined with burgundy felt, and a small mirror had been fitted to the underside of the lid. The box was beautiful—a work of art, each part of it laboriously handcrafted. Noel knocked and came into the cell. He gave me a small slip of paper with the address of a Manchester law firm on it.

'Try writing to these people, Alex, they may be able to help get something done about your case'.
'Noel, thanks'.
'No trouble. See you later'.
'Yeah, man'.

After he'd gone, I looked across at Tony. The only really constructive help I've been given since I was sentenced has been from people like Noel. OK, so he's IRA, which doesn't detract from the quality of his assistance. I've found that the various officials and authorities connected with the government don't want to know me or anything about why I was sentenced. They couldn't give a shit. Yet the people who do want to help, the pressure groups and organizations . . . and individuals . . . tend to be themselves left wing. But if I contact them it's perceived as if I'm behaving particularly badly. If I don't contact them, nothing gets done at all. Is this *Catch 22* or what?

'It's a struggle Alex, I know. The only way to get something done is to construct something with care and patience—like this jewellery box. When I started it, it was just bits of wood. Look at it now. So have patience. Maybe something will be done by the ordinary people one day, but it won't happen just like that. It all takes time . . . '.

My vision of democracy wasn't entirely my own, and it may indeed have had a Soviet influence behind it. For democracy to work there needed to be a true egalitarian base, from which the freedoms could be constructed. This had nothing to do with Communism, or any other 'ism'. Each factory, each school and housing estate, each hospital, could delegate their own agents to represent them at a local level. There was nothing crazy about that. If a town produced a hundred delegates in this way, and if, in turn, those delegates voted for a single representative to go to Parliament then Parliament would be more truly representative of the people.

Each delegate, at both local and national level, could be voted out of office at any time, if the people thought he or she was not managing the job properly. There had to be true accountability. With the present system, a prospective Parliamentary candidate could fool the local electorate, and make a total botch-up of the job over the next four years, if the candidate was successful, without any comebacks at all.

Sometimes I'd leave my cell and lean on the landing-rail outside where I had a good view of the rest of the wing. The cons would come and go, heading for the recess or to a friend's cell. Some were hawking illicit goods, others buying them: radios, drugs, tobacco. The bookie was collecting bets, newspaper racing pages in one hand and a small trannie in the other. His runner followed him around with a pillowcase containing some snout and paper money. Von was walking along the Two's landing with a pisspot. When he saw me watching he waved cheerily.

'Alright Strog?'
'Yea man, still breathing'.

• • •

Crazy Horse, a wiry black geezer with mad eyes reflecting all the abuse he'd inflicted upon himself throughout his brief history leapt out of his doorway into the path of a five-year man, scaring him shitless. Peter Cook was waddling from his cell to the SO's office, no doubt with the latest of a series of complaints, each one petty and insignificant, but excruciatingly important to him. Hard to imagine him as the Cambridge Rapist, a person the whole country had been afraid of a few years previously.

Paddy Hill came out of a cell a few doors away carrying a couple of flasks of hooch. He called out a greeting as he went by. Twenty-two life sentences, man . . . and we all knew he'd been fitted-up. God help us all, I thought. *Woof.*

CHAPTER NINE

My companion from the rooftop, Steve, came over from D-wing one evening, for a chat—and a drop of hooch. My cell stunk like a brewery, the result of a mishap a few days earlier when a bucket of fermenting hooch, wrapped in a black bin-liner, exploded during the night dispersing the contents in a 360 degree spread over all and everything. Nobody was really bothered, least of all the screws. The only time they ever came down heavy-handed, was if a bloke got both drunk and aggressive . . . otherwise, no problem.

Steve scooped out a pint from another bucket, kept under my bed. It was ten days old and quite strong. He had a packet of Bensons on him, and he gave me five out of the packet. We both lit-up and got down to the reason for his visit.

'Another rooftop, Alex. Next week. You interested?'
'Dunno Steve. Depends. What's the SP on it?'
'A protest over the food. It's shit. Up on the wing roof this time'.
'Is it you and me or what?'
'No, there'll be a few of us. We're gonna make a big deal of it. Stay up a few days, sling a few slates, sing a few songs. Ha'.
'Steve, listen. I ain't going to be able to do it'.
'OK'.
'Reasons: it was 'flu for me the last time. It's too soon for me to go again, especially if we got to stay up there for days. And I can't sing songs, I've got a lousy baritone'.
'Ha! Yeah, man. Look, I just thought you might be interested'.

No more was said about it after that. We changed the subject. Tony knocked on the door and walked in—we had a code, if he knocked in a certain way, we'd know it was him. He saw Steve and made to back out again.

'Sorry, I'll come back later . . . '.
'You're alright Tone', Steve said. 'We've finished talking'.
'How's things going?'
'Not too bad Steve . . . Yourself?'
'Same as usual. It's keeping one step ahead, that's the trouble'.

Steve had knocked a couple of screws out over the years, and he was barricaded up most of the time. His cell was an obstacle course . . . when you walked in there was a cupboard you had to step around and there was a table, also placed in the way, to navigate around. And then there was a locker. Once past those obstacles was Steve's bed.

Whenever anything was going down, and a con had to be 'extracted' by the screws, they'd wait until everyone had been banged up, and then go into the man's cell team-handed, and pull him out and drag him away. Because everyone'd been banged-up, there were never any witnesses to give an account of what had happened. Usually it happened during the night, when the con was at his weakest and so unable to resist properly. It had happened to Steve a few times, so now he was playing safe. If his cell door was opened during the night and the screws went in they'd have considerable difficulty getting to his bed. And, when they'd finally managed it, Steve'd be wide-awake and ready for them . . .

Parkhurst rules.

Tony sat down on the end of the bed and Steve scooped a pint of hooch for him out of the bucket.

'So. What's new?', I asked.
'We've got ourselves a bent screw. Says he'll take our letters out the back door and post them for us . . .'.
'Nice of him. Who is it?'
'Harry F from over on C wing'.
'You'll be sorry', Steve said from behind a stream of tobacco smoke.
'I agree'.

I knew of the screw in question and I'd have thought Tony knew the SP on him too. It quickly transpired that he did.

'Yeah'.
'So?'
'Think about it. OK, anything we give him'll go straight to the burglars. Right. But it could work out in our interests . . .'.
'With you', Steve approved. 'Ahead of you'.

Which was when it caught up with me, too. Misinformation. A letter could be written, stating, for example, that something big was due to come down. An escape, a rooftop, whatever. That'd create the diversion, while the genuine action went down some place else. It was a tempting thought . . . but it was something else that was bothering me. How had Harry known that Tony was the person to approach . . . ? That Tony was LHRO? Our reports were compiled with the utmost care and there was always a request that the newspapers the reports were sent to did *not* reveal their source. We always used a two-character code prefix, to guarantee the reports were genuine, and came from us. Only one signature had ever been used . . . Tony's, as secretary to the LHRO. I knew that I was certainly compromised, and had been ever since I took the drug sample to the member of the Board of Visitors. But no-one had proof, only suspicion. Still, Tony wasn't involved in that, so there must be a leak somewhere for them to have made the link. The answer came immediately. Tony and I spent a lot of time together; the screws had simply noted his association with me and put two and two together. Simple. That was the likeliest answer, but there nonetheless remained a doubt, a possibility that a leak might exist. A grass . . .

● ● ●

The membership of the LHRO had increased to eight in Parkhurst, and five others at The Scrubs, Gartree and Albany. Each of the members was of good intelligence and sound integrity. They had involved themselves because of their convictions, in an attempt to do something about a system, which they understood to be particularly unwholesome and corruptive. Each was prepared to see his sentence extended, if need be, because of that involvement, and because of the beliefs each man held. It was also likely that the screws wanted us to know that they were on to us. That would also explain the approach made to Tony.

'Tony. What did the screw say to you exactly?', I asked.
'He said he sympathised with the work we're doing and that if we ever wanted anything taken out of the nick, like a letter for instance, all we had to do was to give it to him and he'd do the job for us'.
'Did he mention any names?' Steve wanted to know.
'No'.
'Tony', I said, 'Go back to him and tell him thanks, but no. That nobody's interested. We don't need it. Let's stick to the routes we already have, they're safe enough'.

When the rooftop protest went down a few days later, it went down with a vengeance . . . It was to be the A and D-wing roof (both wings are joined together). It was a sloping slate roof, typical of the Victorian design, and very difficult to reach, because the drainpipes were cemented in such a way as to render them impossible to climb. It was a high building and anyone attempting a climb from outside, without ropes and hooks, would surely fail. So there had to be another way up. The men decided to go up from the inside of the wing. The interiors of the wings were again of Victorian design, hollow in the middle, with tiers of cells on each side, and a safety net stretched across the lower landing, to catch anyone thrown over the top.

• • •

Natural illumination came from skylights in the roof. These were of glass and protected with a barred grill, to stop anyone from climbing through to the roof. The skylights had no ladders or other means of access. Yet they were the only way of reaching the roof from the inside, so there had to be a way of getting through . . . It was decided that the best bet would be to use a rope and hook, which could be used to catch onto the grill, then perhaps the grill could be pulled loose from below, thereby removing the barrier to the skylight. Once that was done, the hook could be used again, this time to snag the skylight proper and allow the men to climb up and through, one at a time.

It was a daring plan, and one that was fraught with dangers. Once the hook was thrown at the grill, there'd be no turning back. That action in itself constituted at attempt to escape, and the punishment would be severe. Then the climbing of the rope . . . the hook would be a home-made one, and not the kind of thing a skilled climber would trust his life to; for if the hook should slip, or the rope snap, nothing would save the climber from severe injuries or worse. And while all this was going on, what would the screws be doing? It was very clear that the protest wouldn't be about the food. All of the men, except Steve, were IRA, which meant that the protest was going to be political. The gutter press always tried to have it that the IRA prisoners were hated and reviled by the rest of the prison population. The truth was and is the opposite of that. In this case, as soon as the hook was thrown at the skylight grill, the rest of the cons began blocking the iron stairwells, so the screws would be prevented from gaining access to the top floor landing; thus giving the men the time they needed to get the job done.

The operation went without a hitch. The grill was pulled away, and the men, a half a dozen of them, shimmied up the makeshift rope, through the skylight and onto the roof. Thus began the most costly and damaging demonstration Parkhurst had ever seen in the whole of its history. As is always the case in such situations, all of the cons were told to go behind their cell doors and banged up. My cell on B-wing was on the top landing and if I looked out of the window I could see everything going down on the A and D-wing roof opposite. Noel, Paddy and Sean were busy smashing the glass in all of the skylights, shouting, 'Look out below!' I could hear the glass as it hit the floor inside the wings and I knew then that both the wings would have to be evacuated, which meant ship-outs and ghostings. C-wing would have to make room for those who'd not be removed in that way.

After the skylights had been smashed, the men began the task of removing the roof. It's ever so easy for people who read about these things from the comfort of their armchairs to wax lyrical on how convicts who take such action must be whipped, keelhauled and thrown in a dungeon on bread and water for having the audacity to demonstrate and destroy prison property. Such people have not seen the inside of a prison, never mind a strip cell. Nor have they been forced to relinquish control of their lives, or submit themselves to the uniquely British methods of degradation and applied harm which constitute the official definitions of 'punishment'. Logically, any person who has *not* been a prisoner can know absolutely nothing of the experience of being a prisoner. It follows that such a person has no knowledge at all of what motivates a prisoner—no understanding of prison psyche, of the excruciating stresses and strictures imposed upon a free will. The only quality possessed by such a person is ignorance.

This is true also of Home Office ministers and those in their employ and service. I have to say that much trouble with the prison system has been and perhaps still is caused by people who are ignorant of the real effects on prisoners. It's simple enough to construct a cage for a lion and then to poke at it with a whip and a chair, any fool can strive towards that. But, beware of the lion when the fool turns his or her back!

● ● ●

Looking out of my cell window at the men on the opposite roof I felt a profound sadness that fellow human beings are driven to such lengths. If any one of them slipped on that sloping roof it would mean instant death. It wasn't a game. I had thought many times that I would love to destroy prison. Oh yes please—and not just because I am innocent of the crimes I was sent to prison for.

I read once of Rudolph Hess talking, in wonder, about wealthy Chinese who, when fortune was good to them, bought caged birds at market and then opened the cages and let the birds fly away. I feel real emotions for animals in zoos and—rather than pay to go and peer at them—I would tear off the roofs of the cages and buildings and let the animals go free . . . and I would make such a good job of it that the zoo would never be used again to hold captive living creatures. Man's capacity to snare, entrap and imprison is obscene negativity, a symptom of hatred and envy but expressed in a socially permissible way. God loves us all.

When the skylights had been smashed, the work of taking the roof off began. I watched Steve, straddling the apex of the tiled roof, staring at some point out of sight. He swung a leg over and began hammering his heels against the topmost row of tiles. The tiles began to break up and slide down over the edge into space, shattering in the concrete far below. There were loud cheers from cells all over the wings; again, the most hated symbol for prisoners is the prison which holds them captive . . . and any attack on the prison physically is especially sweet. It's seen as a blow for freedom—a shaking of the fist at the faceless ignorant people who need an Official Secrets Act for more reasons than one.

That same evening a fire engine came into the prison, and parked just out of throwing range of the rooftop protesters. It had grown dark outside, and the luminous strips of the firemen's coats shone like yellow striplights. We all of us wondered what was happening. There was no fire. The fire hoses were laid out and connected to hydrants. Wheels were turned. The hoses swelled and . . . We couldn't believe it! The water was aimed at the men on the roof—Sean caught a jet across the chest and almost toppled off the roof at the force of it.

A loud angry roar filled the night as the rest of the cons saw what was happening. Somebody threw a sauce bottle from a cell window, and it hit a fireman over the head . . . Luckily he wore his helmet. More missiles were thrown, and the firemen had to withdraw smartly, winding their hoses up as they went. What we'd witnessed was an attempt to squirt the men off the roof . . . ! The next day, one of the cons told a visitor what had been done, and by the end of the day it was included in a local news report on Radio Victory. 'Official sources', the report said, had denied the allegation. A cover up then. The situation was becoming more tense as each day came and went. The A and D-wing roofs were slowly disappearing as more and more slates were broken up. A skeletal frame was emerging, as the wings were gradually exposed to the elements. Also the screws were becoming ever more paranoid.

• • •

The exercise periods were transferred to an asphalt apron immediately in front of B-wing and we were urged to keep moving by nervous screws with straining alsation dogs on short leashes. Radios crackled constantly as the burglars communicated with the control room. At the first sign of trouble all hell would be let loose. The screws fully expected a riot, and as a result of their managing of the situation it came very close to one. A lighted match would've set it off. Feelings were running so high.

From the vantage point of my cell window, I watched each stage of the rooftop demonstration unfold, until on the sixth day there were no slates left at all. The cons from A and D-wings had indeed been evacuated. Some had been relocated onto C wing, but many others had been Shanghaii'd to the Scrubs, Albany and Gartree.

All of us knew what the demonstrators could expect when they finally came down. The demonstrators themselves also knew it, which was why they were demanding someone from the Board of Visitors to monitor their descent—to guard against retaliation from the screws. Of course, I had no illusions about the Board of Visitors and if it'd been me up there I'd have asked for a media presence with a photographer. The men were told not to come down together, but one at a time.

As each prisoner reached the ground, a posse of screws and governor grades surrounded him, and marched him off out of sight. Later, each of the men alleged that they had been beaten, some severely so, and they were moved from Parkhurst on 'ten-fifty sevens'—otherwise known as 'lay-downs'—meaning four months in one prison, then three months in another prison, and so on, being kept segregated in the blocks with no privileges, and as much sensual deprivation as was permissible.

As for A and D-wings, they were to remain unoccupied for many years until they were finally refurbished at a cost of many millions of pounds. It wasn't long before I was to be moved myself. I was taken off the Category A list in 1980, my last year at Parkhurst. In that year I witnessed a number of changes which were to make the gaol very different to what it had been. New restrictive policies were being put into effect. The new programme included tighter control of inmates' activities across the board; when I was told I was going to be transferred I wasn't sorry at the prospect of leaving.

• • •

I'd met some good people. I'd also met some crazy, weird and evil people. The latter, I have to say were in a very small minority. Not all of the screws were bad; there were some good ones. As in all walks of life, some of them were just indifferent—in the job for the money and security. The bad ones were worse than the prisoners in their charge, but the decent ones—usually the older ones—normally cared enough to make an impression. Those older men had been in the job many years and had more experience, not only of Prisonworld, but also of life in general; I respected most of them. I made an attempt to find out which gaol I was to be transferred to, but the authorities refused to tell me.

As I was no longer a Category A man and Category B instead. I knew I would be moved to a Category B gaol—unfortunately there were many

Cat. B nicks around the country, and there was no way of finding out which one. A few months before leaving Parkhurst one of the cons collapsed a few doors away down the landing; it happened as I was returning from the recess one evening. I thought he was having a fit so I turned him over onto his side and put my jacket under his head. But he came round fairly quickly and it transpired he'd had a dizzy spell and just keeled over . . . I invited him into my cell and made a mug of sweet tea for him. He was a thin stick of a guy and looked as if a smile hadn't hit him for some considerable time. His name was Geoff and he was in for six years, but he didn't tell me why and I didn't ask. Parkhurst rules again.

He said he was on hunger strike, but hadn't told the screws about it. I asked him what he was hoping for and he said he just wanted to die— as simple as that. He must've been in his middle twenties, or middle thirties, it was difficult to tell. His eyes had deep violet half circles beneath them, his skin sallow and covered in spots, his hair was falling out and his breathing was shallow. He'd lost any pride in his appearance; his jacket was too big for him and his jeans were held up by a pair of bootlaces tied together. Of course, those clothes must have fitted him properly before he started on his hunger strike . . .

'Are you drinking, Geoff?'
'A bit'.
'So what's wrong? Why the hunger strike? Look, drink that tea man, before it goes cold'.

I knew the sugar in it'd give him a bit of energy. I didn't speak again. I sat down on the floor with my back to the wall and waited. Sometimes it's best not to say anything. A silence is often as beneficial as words. Slowly, I felt his vibes become less erratic. Looking at him I knew that he didn't have much time in life; all the symptoms of advanced vitamin and mineral deficiency were there. He'd collapsed because his battery had gone flat. I rolled a couple of cigarettes and gave him one. After a short while we both became harmonious within our silence and became as one, an empathy was born, a peace. A plain had been found way above Prisonworld, a plain where it was safe to speak out without fear and where the understanding was total.

'I can't handle this place. I'm in the wrong prison. I don't know why I was sent here because I'm not doing my bird for anything serious. I can't get visits because I'm from South Shields and it's too far for my parents to travel. Every night I'm afraid of what the next day will bring, I sleep but I don't sleep—can you understand that?'

'Aye, Geoff . . . '
'My girlfriend's on the Social. She can't travel this far either and I know I'm losing her. Maybe I've already lost her. She used to write to me a lot, but now my letters aren't being answered at all. I love her and I don't know what to do . . . I've been to see the welfare officer but he says there's nothing he can do'.

That, of course, was a story I'd heard so often. Most of the trouble caused in prison was down to guys getting 'Dear John' letters sent to them. There was no love in prison, only brutilisation of the senses. Prisoners became desperate for word from their wives and girlfriends, for words of love, of sympathy and understanding. For some men, letters to and from loved ones were the only things that got them through. Being sent to prison was a way of saying 'Society's given up on you. Nobody wants to know anymore'. To have one's wife or girlfriend say the same compounded the trauma.

The prison system has a way of sending convicted men to the furthest prison from their own area. The case with Geoff was typical. A man from as far away as South Shields, being made to serve his sentence in a prison on the Isle of Wight! Such a crazy situation made it impossible for a working class partner to visit with any regularity, if at all. I was from Lancashire myself and my mother could only visit twice in the six years I'd been on the Island. She had to ask for a photograph to know what I looked like . . . No blame should be directed at partners for sending 'Dear John' letters. Who could blame them? A geezer gets sent down for ten years and it's not supposed to affect the relationship? Alice in Wonderland again. Some women stood by their men throughout, but it takes a special kind of lass to do that. The pressures are so heavy. As for this lad, Geoff, what could I tell him? To stop harming himself. Easy to come out with the clichés. He'd probably heard them all himself and even likely that he'd tried to reason them out. But he hadn't had much success had he?

'Alright Geoff, I'll tell you what to do. First of all, don't die. There ain't no future in it man. Careful, Geoff you nearly smiled for a second. If you die there ain't no coming back. If you really love your girlfriend I doubt if you'd want to have her weeping her heart out at your graveside, yes? So think about not what's best for you, but what's best for her . . . Write her a letter, telling her that she doesn't have to write back, that you understand the way of it, but that you want to write, to keep her up to date on how you are. Even tell her you don't mind her going out with a geezer, if that's what she wants. Be realistic man, you won't be in prison forever. There's still grass out there, and flowers and leaky bus shelters, and fish an' chip suppers, and cans of beer, if that's what you're into. I can make you a very sincere promise, Geoff. *Woof*— and it's this: In six months' time you'll be bloody glad you didn't give in now.

'How long are you doing?'
'Six years?'
'Well, that's bed and breakfast. If you're interested, I'll introduce you to someone who's serving 22 life sentences. Yes? I'm serious. And you know what? I'll tell you, he's innocent. What about that?'

Well, in the end Geoff didn't die. I got him to be too interested in his life. One day, I said, he'd be a happily married man with a wife and a family. But, as with all people who've been on the hunger strike, his body never got back to normal—not to how it should've been. That for him—and for many others—was Prisonworld's legacy. A souvenir of hell.

CHAPTER TEN

I was told I would be leaving Parkhurst—not to go to a Category B prison after all but making a sideways move to another dispersal gaol. When I asked why I was being moved to another top-security prison no one could come up with an answer. A sideways move, which worked out as equal to another two years to serve. It was outrageous. Although none of the staff could find a reason for the move, they nevertheless warned me to accept it, because there wasn't anything anyone could do. If I complained, well, it may make things worse. I didn't think anything could make things any worse than they were, but that was me being negative again. Another two years could be spent on an Open University course and, after all, two years isn't exactly an eternity, is it? Think positive! Yeah man.

The gaol I was going to was Gartree. It'd just had a riot, but I was assured it was a less restrictive nick with a relatively open programme of activities. If this was meant to reassure me, it didn't. I'd never heard of a gaol becoming 'less restrictive'—just after a riot—before! The opposite is always the case. I was told I'd probably be moving within a month or so, but true to form they wouldn't tell me exactly when. This to was to stop me contacting some blithe spirit on the Out who could spring me en route from the escort. And so, as each day went by, I woke up thinking it'd be the last day of my stay there. I kept packing and unpacking my cardboard box, so often that the cardboard was wearing thin. People were coming to say 'goodbye' every day.

'Bloody Hell, Strog, you ain't half got the lot of us going . . .', Von complained.
'It's not my bloody fault is it? Stop complaining'.
'Trouble is', Chill said, 'Gartree don't want you an' they're tryin' to find someplace that does'.

Joe gave me a kettle, a Seiko automatic, and a gold-plated bracelet.

'This isn't for you to wear it's to trade-up for snout when you get there, OK?'

It was thoughtfully done. I went years of listening to Cockneys calling wrist watches 'kettles' before I found out why. Joe had explained: 'It's rhyming slang, innit? Kettle on the Hob. Hob, fob. Fob watch. Yeah? Gaw struth . . .'.

Clive Duck and Dive came 'round, with a Grundig Yacht Boy radio.

'Hey Alex. Somethin' for you, mate'.

Crazy Horse surprisingly, gave me a flick knife. Shit, I thought. 'What do I want this for man?' Secretly, I was pleased. Very few people ever had it with him because, well, he was an original. He was a loner among loners. No one ever got close to him. I'd hardly spoken to him, and here he was slipping a flick-knife into my jacket pocket! In his way he was giving me what he thought I'd need to keep myself well-protected and safe. It was some gesture . . .

'For you to sharpen your pencils', he answered—and was gone.

I gave the knife to Chilly and asked him to get rid. If the burglars had decided to search me and found the knife I'd have lost something like five years and been put back on Category A . . .
  When you're on the inside doing bird, it's often difficult to know who your friends are . . . but you always find out when you're leaving the nick. The people who come to wish you well, give you a packet of snout, who make sure you've got the small letters of introduction—each one written on a fag-paper—so you've got a contact at the new place. Apart from other cons, a couple of the screws saw me all right for snout, too . . .

'Survive. And *reach* people!', the ghost of Nobby Clarke kept whispering to me.

Well, it looked as though I'd made it through Parkhurst anyway. I'd got in touch with the firm of solicitors Noel had recommended. They'd go so far into the case, then begin meeting brick walls; any demands to the Home Office for information were simply ignored. I didn't know at the time, but a file on me was kept at the Home Office. Someone later told me that I had to do 30 years before I could get out . . . ![1] Little wonder, then, that solicitors had such a bad time extracting information of any sort—because it wasn't just the one firm who'd tried on my behalf, but more than half a dozen since I'd been sentenced.
  If the authorities wanted me to do 30 years, or, in other words, the equivalent of a 45 year determinate sentence, then Heaven knows what had been said about me . . . this was longer than George Blake had been given . . . ! Thirty years was double or more than what the Train Robbers had to serve—and almost triple what mandatory lifers convicted of murder were spending inside before being released. But at

---

[1]   See the references to Bill Jarvis at p.11 and p. 108

the time I didn't know about the 30 years recommendation—that was only to come out many years later, when I'd reached the 20 years served mark.

Because of my own experiences at the hands of British justice I had a very passionate and genuine desire to highlight acts of judicial miscarriage, and to try and help in their exposure. Whenever I came upon any kind of injustice something happened inside me and I just couldn't let it pass. I'd learned that no system was perfect . . . the trouble with the British was that they believed their system was *perfect!*

Every system has its grey areas where wrongs prevail and which are hidden away from prying eyes. The places of human containment, the prisons and the mental health hospitals, the old peoples' homes, the children's homes and approved schools, these were places which constituted Britain's grey areas. If light was going to permeate to those areas the torches had to be wielded with courage and determination and persistence. This had to be done without compromise.

Just before I was to leave Parkhurst, Tony relinquished the job as secretary to the LHRO. I took over, not realising the group had less than 18 months left to exist before the pin-stripes came down heavy.

CHAPTER ELEVEN

I ought to have been feeling glad to leave Albany and Parkhurst behind but, strangely, I felt a sadness. I guess it was because I'd spent so long at Parkhurst—it'd become a kind of second home, and it was true that I was going to miss a lot of sound people. For the first time I was being transferred as a normal prisoner, and not as an A-Man. The prison bus left the island with half a dozen convicts aboard, plus five screws and the driver. I was cuffed-up to a guy from Watford doing a ten stretch for a series of burglaries back in 1975, or so he said. He was being transferred to The Scrubs, on his own request, because it was nearer for his relatives to visit him there. The bus stopped at Kingston Prison in Portsmouth to pick up a couple of prisoners. At that time Kingston was a prison which only accepted 'domestic' lifers, those who'd killed their partners, usually in the course of domestic arguments. Some countries have a term covering such killings—'Crimes of Passion'. By and large, domestic lifers spend less time in gaol than any type of lifer.

• • •

After leaving Portsmouth there was one other stop, a refreshment break for the screws, at Leatherhead police station. As the bus pulled in at the police station, the bloke I was 'cuffed-up to, gave me a nudge with his elbow; when I looked down, I saw that his hand was free . . . he's slipped the handcuffs. I spat on my wrist and tried to slip my hand too, but I couldn't get them past the wristbone. Unfortunately for us, the principal officer had stood up at the front of the bus, and was checking the handcuffs, before he'd let anyone off. So my travelling companion pushed his hand back into the handcuffs. If he hadn't, he'd've been well and truly nicked and I'd've been put back on the A List.

The PO saw that our 'cuffs were a bit loose, so he stopped us, and tightened the bloody things up. The end of the journey was Wormwood Scrubs, a gaol that a few years later the governor would publicly condemn as a 'human dustbin'. In the reception area I was told that I'd be 'lodging' there for a week, before making the final stage of my journey to Gartree gaol on the Scottish 'National' the following Tuesday. The official days allocated for the mass movement of prisoners around the country were always Tuesdays and Wednesdays. These were the days the prison buses set off from the London nicks in all directions, for example prisoners being transferred from The Scrubs to Barlinnie gaol in Scotland would be moved on the Scottish 'National'. It would stop at Wandsworth first, to pick up more prisoners, then set off Northwards, making intermediate stops along the way either to drop prisoners off or to pick them up. Other buses left London in other directions.

The Liverpool 'National' stopped at Onley YP prison outside Rugby, then went on to call at Winson Green gaol in Birmingham and Strangeways in Manchester. Sometimes it'd stop at Stafford gaol, if anyone needed dropping off, or picking up. It wouldn't arrive at Liverpool gaol until late in the night. Reverse journeys, would either set off the day before, or the day after. A week's stay at The Scrubs was no great hardship.

The main thing was to have enough snout, to cover the stay, because prisoners are never paid while they're 'in transit'. Luckily, I'd been seen all right before leaving Parkhurst, so my time at the gaol was spent mostly reading and sleeping the hours away. So-called 'lodgers' were never given work, because they weren't staying in the prison long enough and it was virtually a 23-hour bang up every day. There was an LHRO representative at The Scrubs, but he was over on the long-term wing, and I never got a chance to go and see him. However, a package was put in my cell one day, when I was out on exercise, containing more tobacco and matches, and a hand-written LHRO report about one of the lifers who'd been refused permission to attend his brother's funeral. I wasn't due a visit while I was at The Scrubs, so I had to take the report with me, and have it taken out when I reached Gartree. Gartree top-security prison was, like Albany, Parkhurst, Wakefield, The Scrubs, Hull and Long Lartin, a dispersal prison. As I have said, my transfer was a sideways move rather than a progressive one (normally a prisoner transferred from a dispersal was given less-secure gaol, a Category B) but all the Home Office was doing in my case was moving me from one dispersal to another. I felt pissed off about it, because only a few months earlier I'd been taken off the A List and made into a Category B prisoner . . . entitling me to a Category B gaol I thought. I'd been told that's what'd happen in fact. So the system wasn't doing me any favours. Again it was reneging on me, going back on its word.

• • •

Gartree gaol was (and still is) a modern gaol, in the sense that its buildings are of redbrick, and to a 'sixties design. It was almost a duplicate of Albany, on the Island, the only material differences, being the lack of close-circuit cameras on the landings and the method of banging up; in Albany, the cell doors were all on an electric system, with intercoms in the cells, but at Gartree everything was mechanical. The cells were all single ones, but had no integral sanitation facilities. The old Victorian system of 'slopping-out' applied. After a couple of weeks of getting to know the place, I felt more or less at home there—after all one prison was the same as any other at the end of the day. There were some familiar faces: Sean Kinsella was there, his black beard streaked with grey now, and still the Provisional Sinn Fein Commandant responsible for the well-being of the Irish prisoners. The last time I'd seen him was almost a year earlier, when he and other Irishmen were taking the roof off A and D-wings at Parkhurst.

An old friend, Gary Beecham was also there. He'd been ghosted out of Parkhurst with George Wilkinson, for taking a screw hostage a couple of years before. I was appalled at the state he was in, the system had reduced him almost to a zombie-like condition, by filling him with disabling drugs, which as far as I could see he didn't need, but were given to stop him from motoring about normally. I wrote to Rose Murray (Art Director of Burnbake Art—a charitable trust set up to encourage prisoners to write, paint and use their time constructively, in a whole range of different ways) and she sent him a record player. A human touch, that, and typical of Rose. There were also one or two faces I recognised. I was still writing to F, although my letters were becoming increasingly emotional and I was beginning to feel a hopelessness about the lack of movement around my case. My letters couldn't have made easy reading, and I began to think of a way to stop the correspondence with her. She deserved better from me. Letters were not supposed to put the reader on a downer, but I knew that's what mine were doing. At that time I believed I'd never get out of prison, ever.

I went to work in the light textiles shop. I had to work different types of sewing machines, starting off on a 'flatbed', in the manufacture of gym vests and prison T-shirts. After a week of it, all the motions came automatically, until I could've done the job blindfold. From then onwards, the job became a mindless one. The workshop, full of sewing machines, was a very noisy place, but after a while it seemed to become less so as the sounds began to work as an anaesthetic on the mind, deadening it. There were around 30 or 40 men working in the shop. The half dozen Irishmen had a corner to themselves. Here, no work was done at all, because the refused to co-operate with the system. I don't think any of them were smokers, so going without wages can't have been as bad as it would otherwise have been. Still, it meant that they had a fairly frugal existence of it. Civilian visitors to Gartree—Home Office officials, probation officers, criminology or sociology students, magistrates etc.—would all be given a grand tour of the place. Often they'd be escorted around the workshops. Whenever they came into ours, the shop instructors would go and shake their hands, and tell them what an industrious lot we were. Just look at all the prisoners, working away at their sewing machines, hardly any trouble, and just look at the quality of these garments . . . Bullshit!

There was always a con who'd brown-nose, usually the same one every time: the shop instructor would escort the visitors around the workshop, and then, suddenly, he'd stop beside the con and say to the visitors:

'Let's ask this man what he thinks of working in here . . . '.

And the con would go,

'A good job this, it's the saving of me, I'll go out and be able to make something of my life now, Guv. I can't thank the prison enough . . .'.

Once in a while the shop instructor would stop beside a different con . . .

'Let's ask this man . . .'
'Fuck off!'

On the wings, there were cooking facilities provided where a man could fry up a pan of hash, or a few eggs. The main kitchen cooked all the prison's meals, but the cookers on the wings were there so that a con could cook up items bought out of his wages, from the prison canteen. Wages were around three quid a week.

One evening, I was in the TV room, watching some programme or other. One of the cons, Heavy Metal, came in with a chip pan full of boiling fat. He poured it over the head of a man who was seated in front of me, who let out a high-pitched, almost silent, scream, as he clawed at his face and hair. The other men told the geezer to shut up. Two days later, I was over the hospital block and I saw the guy with his canister wrapped in bandages, with just tiny holes for the eyes, nose and mouth. The other cons were calling him 'Fritter'. Heavy Metal was given an extra five years to add to his sentence.

• • •

I met up with The Preacher again at Gartree; he was only a few cells away from me on the same landing. He'd got himself a record player, and some magic sounds . . . Grateful Dead, Jefferson Airplane, Joan Baez . . . *Woof*, Lynnyrd Skynnrd. I went around to see him most evenings, and it was like dropping into a time-warp, dope smoke, candles, brother with long, tied-back hair, and a budgie, which hardly ever got off its back, except to stretch its wings and nibble some millet, because the smoke got it stoned. It was called Hawk. And Joan Baez right there on the same wavelength, voicing thoughts that travelled around the cell, and hit the people and knocked them out. The Preacher was into his thirties, but small, wiry-built. His hair was long and his beard shaggy, and his eyes threw wisdom at you. The screws couldn't deal with him, because he fazed them out. Like telling Ghandi he wouldn't get out unless he obeyed every order without question. The Preacher could transform words into glances. He could say to a screw 'Fuck off, you stupid moron!' without opening his mouth. He could talk in the language of nature, converse with flowers.

'You should stop goin' round that geezer's pad Alex', Old George told me once. 'His canister's fucked'.
'No it ain't. Preacher and me, we go back a long way . . .'.
'Well, that's my advice. You don't want to go an' get y'self mixed up with an old hippie like that . . .'.
'George. Listen. It could be a lot worse—he could be an old Tory . . .!
'Bloody weirdos'. Old George was an old Tory.

The preacher, without him knowing it, got my own canister sorted out at a time when it could've gone the other way. There wasn't really anyone else I could relate to, except him, and he taught me a lot. He sat cross-legged on a corner of his cot, strumming an old acoustic guitar. Every now and then he'd break into intricate finger exercises, using the whole of the fretboard, the sounds like a shower of needles falling onto an anvil. The guitar had to be unwrapped from its case and left for a while so it could breathe before he'd play it.

'You see this instrument?', he asked me.
'Sure, it's a guitar'.
'No, it's part of a tree. Yes?' This with an eyebrow raised.
'That's true'.
'Of course it's true! Do you really see what's around you? Or are you asleep?'
'I'm not asleep man. You're right, but so am I. The instrument is a guitar . . .'
'No! It's become a guitar, yes—but you're reading on a superficial level, you need to read deeper! Without doubt the instrument is part of a tree. Yes? Nothing happens by itself. The book on the shelf there is also part of a tree, as is the shelf. Learn to see things as they really are man, before you do anything else. That's important'.

He put the guitar back into its case, the beads of his friendship bands clinking on his thin wrist. In my own cell, I'd sit on the cot and reassess everything within sight. Everyday objects took on new meanings, as I traced their sources. The Preacher was right . . . I'd been asleep, complacent. Within a short time I had developed a different level of perception. Things which I had taken for granted became less so, their significance re-defined. In this way, I learned to look below the surface. I discovered other worlds, both without and within myself, and began to understand the ancient command 'Know thyself!'

'Because you got to start with yourself man', The Preacher intoned, 'before you attempt to understand anythin' else. If you don't know your own self you won't know shit. Have a roll-up . . .'.

• • •

One day I had a letter from a friend from the Church of Scientology. He wanted to come to visit me. The Scientologists helped to fund an organization called the Citizens' Commission on Human Rights; it was set up specifically to monitor drug abuse in the prisons, and was particularly critical of the way prison doctors prescribed drugs for purposes of control, as opposed to legitimate medical treatment. Over the previous couple of years I had been sending the CCHR copies of all the reports drawn-up by the LHRO (the League for Human Rights Observance) at Parkhurst.

Mike, the Scientologist, wanted to come to see me for a chat, but I was told by the assistant governor that I wouldn't be allowed to see him. No reason was given. I pointed out that Mike hadn't ever been in trouble with the law, so there was no reason for preventing him from visiting me. But the assistant governor stood his ground—he'd made his decision and no prisoner was going to get him to change it. Yet the decision was so outrageous I just couldn't let it drop like that.

'Governor, you haven't told me why you're stopping the man from visiting me. You're inferring that my friend is not of good character, and this without you ever having met him. I realise I can't do anything to get you to overturn what you've decided but I've got to tell you that I'm going to challenged it. You're well out of order'.

I spent a couple of days drafting a letter, which I sent to the European Court of Human Rights, at Strasbourg. A reply came back within a week, the tone of the letter was encouraging: that court would take up the case.

The LHRO rep at Gartree was a ten-year man called Joe. He'd been transferred from Parkhurst a year or so earlier, where he'd been a valuable part of the team there. While he'd been at Gartree, he'd got another five men interested in the LHRO and, between them, they'd managed to forge links with the other dispersal gaols, so that messages could go backwards and forwards, faster in some cases than the service provided on the outside by the GPO. Both Joe and I worked in the textiles shop. One day, during a tea break in the afternoon, someone gave him a copy of *The Sun* newspaper; it contained an extensive article featuring the latest 'Yorkshire Ripper' attack.

'Fuckin' sickenin' innit. Makes you weep. It's a monster what's doin' it'.

I could only agree with that.

'The Old Bill aren't doing so well either, they ain't got a clue'.

The civilian shop instructor came over, and pointed out the tea break was over, and we'd better get back to work. But later that day, in the evening, I called for a meeting with Joe and the rest of the Gartree group.

'I've been thinking fella's. Why don't we do something to help get the bastard off the streets . . .'
'So?'
'The Ripper, man'.
'Shit', Joe said with a laugh. 'Ha, So how're we supposed to do that, eh?'
'There's got to be somebody out there who knows him an' what he's up to'.

One of the other geezers, a lifer, spoke up.

'What're you saying Alex? That we find whoever it is ourselves?'
'Aye'.
'But that's impossible!'
'Well, like I said, I've been thinking. There is a way. We appeal to the underworld . . .'
'How?'
'By getting the appeal written-up, sent to a national newspaper and splashed on the front page'.

The appeal wasn't difficult to write, and I'd finished it in half an hour. It had to be written in a certain way, using the language and terminology spoken by prisoners. The difficulty was in getting the document on its way to the newspapers, because it had to go to certain prisoners for their signatures . . . and those prisoners were scattered around five different gaols . . . located at different points of the compass, all over the country. The task we'd set ourselves seemed almost an impossible one, but like most of the other work done by the LHRO every effort was put into the realisation of it. Within a couple of days the appeal was on its way to Long Lartin gaol for two signatures, then onto The Scrubs, and then down to the Island. It took only ten days for the document to arrive back at Gartree. All this had been achieved using methods unique to us. Legitimate channels were avoided. The document never went in the post. During those ten days the LHRO operated more efficiently than the GPO!

Joe and I held a brief meeting, to decide which of the national 'papers the document was to be sent to. In the end, we settled on the *Daily Mirror*, because most prisoners recognised it as being more genuinely concerned with social injustices than any of the Tory-backed newspapers. The appeal was duly sent on its way to the *Mirror* the next day, the last act of the LHRO during the decade of the 'seventies. The eve of 1980 was so celebrated.

A couple of days later, in the first week of the 1980s, the *Mirror* gave the appeal front-page coverage. A banner headline read: 'GRASS ON THE RIPPER!' We held our breath. The next day the Ripper was caught. Although the police might never publicly admit it, their version of the arrest of Peter Sutcliffe may not reveal everything.

● ● ●

At around this time there were many allegations of abuse by prison officers, including one where a man was arrested for minor criminal damage to his girlfriend's flat. He was remanded in custody to his local gaol. The story went that one evening, to cheer himself up a bit, he began singing a few songs. The screws came to his door and told him to belt-up or they'd take him down the block and give him a kicking. But he didn't belt-up. He obviously knew nothing of being in prison and couldn't believe the screws were serious. He continued to sing and the screws came for him. They marched him off down the block where he was thrown into a cell. Outraged, he began to sing again, so his cell door was thrown open, and the screws came in for him. He was later found dead in his cell.

At Wormwood Scrubs gaol, some of the long-termers asked to see the governor about a minor grievance. The men were told to come back the next day. As a result, the men on the long-term wing decided to have a peaceful sit-down protest. Some men sat outside their cells, playing chess or cards, others sat around the television set, or on the floor of the One's (the ground-floor landing). A few hours later, a great noise was heard, beyond one of the access gates to the wing. The gate was unlocked and a great crowd of screws burst through, dressed in riot gear. These screws were armed with various weapons, including heavy boots, and baton sticks of varying lengths; the long-term men were waded into and attacked. None of the prisoners offered a violent response. The next day, the media broadcast a tentative news report, saying that there had been a disturbance at Wormwood Scrubs.

There was no immediate report, stating numbers of casualties. During the next few days, the reports changed, as more news became known . . . the Home Secretary admitted that a handful of prisoners had been hurt. The news station challenged this, saying there was a rumour that many more than 'a handful' of men had been injured. The Home Office denied this. Over the next couple of weeks, the Home Office made various statements, admitting that the casualties numbered more than a handful. There were 20 . . . then there were 30 . . . and then there were more. In the end it was admitted that the numbers of injured prisoner numbered 80 or more. The public were thus given a brief period of reflection, during which it was implicitly understood, that the authorities subjected the people in its care to acts of violence. The incident at The Scrubs should've done what the Strangeways incident did almost a decade later . . . it ought to have precipitated a major inquiry into the methods used by the Home Office and the Prison Department. This was when we needed a Woolf Report, and a Judge Tumim Report. This was when we most needed, a focusing of national attention towards the system. However, the authorities engaged in a classic campaign of misinformation and cover-up; this, coupled with that intransigence unique to British government, ensured that the crisis in the system was diluted, and misdirected towards the prisoners themselves, so that it appeared to the public that the prisoners were themselves wholly responsible. The Home Office, incredibly, concluded by asking for more powers to crush the rebellious prisoners, and to initiate a tighter control on prison regimes!

• • •

One day, at lunchtime, I was told to pick up a letter from the censor's office. Usually, incoming mail was given out by the screw in charge of the landing (the landing officer)—so I knew straightaway that something was up. When I got to the censor's office, I was given a large brown paper envelope; inside was a brief letter saying that a booklet was enclosed. But there was no sign of the booklet.

'Boss, there's supposed to be a booklet with this letter . . .'.
'That's right', the censor said. 'But you'll have to make an application to the governor. It's been stopped'.
'What? Well can I see the booklet so at least I know what it is?'

He held up a booklet for me to see. It was called *The Liquid Cosh*. At last the Parkhurst LHRO reports had been published! But why was I being stopped from having it in my possession . . . ?

'Well', the censor explained, 'it's inflammatory literature'.
'Right, Well I'm going to make a request to see the governor tomorrow morning'.

The next morning I duly made an application, at the wing office, to be seen by the governor. Just before lunch I was called-up and was told the governor would see me. So, I went along to the designated office. The governor sat behind a table with screws around the room at various points, the usual set-up.

'Governor, I had a book sent to me yesterday but the censor told me I couldn't have it. I had to see you about it. Can you do anything to clear this up . . . ?"
'Ah. Alexandrowicz. Yes I'm aware of the book, I'm afraid you can't have it'.
'But why not?'
'Come on. I think you know why not. I'm not prepared to allow inflammatory material into my prison'.
'I can't agree that it's inflammatory governor'.

He'd already made up his mind, and I knew that I wasn't going to shift him. So I had to think fast.

'I'm one of the writers involved in the booklet; I'd like to see it in case anything's been attributed to me that shouldn't . . . '

He thought for a moment.

'I'll allow you to see it for ten minutes only and in the company of a prison officer'.

That was it. Ten minutes, supervised. Not much of a concession, but at least I'd be able to view the pages. A few hours later, I was told to report to one of the wing offices where I found a screw sitting at a table reading the book. When I went in he looked up and said the ten minutes were beginning now. There was too short a time to read the whole thing properly, so I quickly glanced though the pages, to get an idea of the argument it presented, and how it was presented.

The booklet was published by the Church of Scientology for the Citizen's Commission on Human Rights (an international human rights organization sponsored by the C of S to investigate forms of abuse in prisons—in this instance drugs dished out by prison doctors). Of course, the content of the book may have touched off a protest or two, had it been available to the cons. But that was but a possibility, not a probability. Still, I understood where the governor was coming from; he was playing safe.

I told Joe about the booklet after I'd had my ten minutes, so that he could pass on the news to other LHRO workers, in other prisons. The booklet was very hard-hitting. It'd been contributed to by a doctor, and by CCHR representatives. In all, it comprised a grave indictment against the system, and was the first publication I'd ever seen to do that. I'd read a book by Jessica Mitford called *The American Prison Business* which described how prisoners were often given experimental drugs, so that the drugs could be tested and their effects analysed. It demonstrated how prisoners were used as human guinea pigs, by the unscrupulous system . . . but nothing had been written about the British system, so *The Liquid Cosh* was something of a breakthrough. Much of the text was written by me, and credited to me. There was my photograph also. This was the first time I'd become 'visible' to the Home Office; all LHRO reports, when sent to the media, asked for confidentiality. This ensured that whoever wrote the report would be protected from any possible repercussions. But, with the publication of *The Liquid Cosh*, the cat was well and truly out of the bag—as far as I was concerned.

Sure enough, a couple of weeks later, I was paid a visit by a Home Office official who warned me to wind up the LHRO. Failure to do that would result in our sentences being extended . . . My immediate reaction was to say 'Go to Hell!'—but the rest of the men would have to be consulted. During the exercise period, the next day, Joe and I had a lengthy discussion. Some of the LHRO men were serving fixed sentences, and stood to lose the chance of parole if they continued their work. No doubt they would stand firm, even with such a threat hanging over them, but they had responsibilities to their wives, girlfriends and families to get out of prison in the shortest time possible. This became the overriding factor. I gave up my position as secretary to the LHRO, and drew up a letter, to be circulated, stating that, because of Home Office pressure, the LHRO was to be wound up. To their credit, most of the LHRO men continued for long afterward, working with other groups in the cause of establishing justice in their gaols, and in the monitoring of human rights. None of us thought the LHRO had been ineffective; rather, it was felt that we had made effective and significant progress.

The LHRO closed down on 2 February1981.

After the Chronicles End

David Wilson

CHAPTER ONE

A Descriptive Outline

A male life sentenced prisoner will not spend all of his sentence in one, or even two prisons. Instead he will move around the country depending on the reports made on him by prison staff, which in turn will ultimately affect his security classification. Sometimes these reports are concerned with attempting to get him to learn a specific skill, or undertake a specialised course that is seen as being beneficial. These in turn will determine whether or not the prisoner is seen as being ready for parole. On the other hand these reports may be more negative, and the move, or 'transfer'—as it is known within the prison service—a result of the prisoner attempting to escape, or following some falling out either with the prison staff or other prisoners.

Much of what Alex describes in relation to the prisons he was transferred to, and the experiences which he had, whilst unique and arresting nonetheless also follow an emerging pattern of how a lifer would be 'managed' through his 'career' as a life sentenced prisoner. As a consequence it would be helpful to spend a little time describing more generally how such prisoners are dealt with by HM Prison Service, and flagging up issues related to *discretionary* as opposed to *mandatory* life sentenced prisoners. These differences become crucial to Alex's case— most notably in relation to how he was eventually released, which will be dealt with in a subsequent chapter. Thereafter this chapter describes the numbers and types of prisons that Alex spent time in, and uses documentary evidence to suggest some of the themes that would haunt Alex through the remainder of his sentence.

• • •

The sentence of life imprisonment has existed for some time, but with the abolition of capital punishment it became the only sentence available to the courts for the offence of murder. This is known as the *mandatory* life sentence. However at the discretion of the sentencing judge, life imprisonment can be imposed on numerous other offences, as it was in Alex's case. This use of the *discretionary* life sentence dates back to the 1950s, and tends to be imposed for manslaughter, buggery, rape, and arson, but also seems to have been developed as a form of preventative detention for offenders who were perceived as unstable or dangerous. Thus it would appear that punishment was not the sole reason for the sentence being passed. However in 1968 the Court of Appeal identified the criteria that had to be met before a judge could pass a discretionary life sentence. These were that the offence or the offences have to be in themselves serious enough to warrant a very long sentence; that the person convicted of these offences is unstable and might commit further offences; and, finally, when, if the offences are committed, the consequences to other people may be especially serious. Far from following these guidelines, it became clear that judges started to use the discretionary life sentence in circumstances that would not have attracted a very long determinate sentence, as outlined by the Court of Appeal in 1968. Discretionary life sentences were thus being imposed on offenders who would normally have expected a determinate sentence of, say, three or four years—and this fact was to become particularly important when European legislation started to have an impact on the British judicial process.

As a consequence, the numbers of life sentenced prisoners—both mandatory and discretionary—applied to both men and women in England and Wales increased year on year. By the time that Alex was released, for example, the number of life sentenced prisoners was exactly 3,000, representing around seven per cent of the total prison population, of whom 79 per cent were serving mandatory life sentences for murder. No other European prison system has to cope with these numbers, and a study of this issue in the 1990s suggested that the United Kingdom had more life sentenced prisoners than the rest of the European Community put together. These numbers have continued to rise, and by 1997, for example, the most recent year for which we have statistical information, the number of life sentenced prisoners had increased to 3,721, of whom all but 137 were men.[1]

---

[1] For a comprehensive account, including the creation, since 1997, of an additional type of mandatory life sentence (for various repeated serious offences), see *Murderers and Life Imprisoment*, Eric Cullen and Tim Newell, Waterside Press, 1999

A LIFER'S 'CAREER'

To a greater or lesser degree all life sentences are 'planned'. Just after Alex's *Prison Chronicles* end, and partly in response to changes initiated in 1983 by Leon Brittan—at the time Home Secretary—a new system was introduced concerning how life sentenced prisoners were managed. In short, as the Home Secretary now wanted to determine the date of the lifer's first review, in consultation with the trial judge, on the basis of the 'requirements of retribution and deterrence', new systems for coping with these changes had to be put into place by HM Prison Service. As a result, all adult male life sentenced prisoners came under the central management of the Lifer Management Unit (LMU) in DSP2 Division at Prison Service Headquarters, Cleland House in London. Initially the LMU had just two prison governors working within it, and this fact caused criticism given that there was a considerable number of life sentenced prisoners within the penal system, who quite rightly felt that they might serve longer in custody than would otherwise be the case because of administrative overload. Nonetheless this was the system that Alex had to deal with, and whether it was efficient or not he would be judged as suitable for release on the basis of the planning that was expected within his sentence and—as the Brittan changes suggest—within the context of growing political interest in who should get released, and when.

Stages of a life sentence

There are four main stages of a life sentence, which are intended to meet the changing needs of the system, and the lifers themselves. Following the imposition of a life sentence it was usual for a lifer to be allocated to a main lifer centre, such as HMPs Wormwood Scrubs or Wakefield—where Alex was himself allocated. Normally someone of Alex's age (then 18) would not have been allocated to an adult prison, but perhaps the fact that he was a Category A prisoner determined the choices available. At the main lifer centre various initial reviews and reports, known as F75s—the name refers to the number of the form that the report is written on—are prepared, and these are then forwarded to DSP2, who would determine the next move that had to be made. The second stage is usually the longest part of the life sentence, and can be served at more than one prison, but is usually served at a dispersal prison or in a Category B 'training' prison. It is at this stage that the lifer is supposed to 'address' his offending behaviour by engaging in counselling groups, or gaining qualifications, or work experience. In doing so the lifer will, in theory, be viewed as less of a 'risk', but this can be tested out during the third and fourth stages of the life sentence.

The third stage involves re-allocating the prisoner to a Category C prison, which is often described by prisoners as very stressful indeed. This stress is in part caused by the fact that the accommodation available in most Category C prisons is dormitory accommodation, which, by its very nature, involves a loss of privacy. This in turn often makes the lifer who has become used to the security of being able to shut himself in his cell away from the tensions and rivalries of the wing anxious about 'watching his back'—protecting himself from attack. Not only that, the nature of his fellow prisoners has changed. In all likelihood the lifer will now be mixing with prisoners serving relatively short sentences, and he will have to become accustomed to watching people come and go as they reach their release date. This inevitably produces mixed feelings of dread and longing. The fourth stage is when, with the approval of the minister of state at the Home Office, the life sentenced prisoner is moved to an open prison, as a Category D prisoner. As part of the process of being in the open prison the lifer will be given home leaves, or supervised days, and then unsupervised days, out of the prison. Finally, some time prior to release, the prisoner might also be asked to go into a Pre-elease Employment Scheme hostel, where the lifer will be expected to find work in the community, and save a certain amount of his wages.

The life sentenced prisoner will then be released, but that is not the end of the story. Such a prisoner is regarded as being on life licence, and this special form of licence is supervised by the Probation Service in the area where the lifer intends to live. The life licence remains in force, literally for life, and can be revoked at any given time if the supervising probation officer believes that the lifer is giving cause for concern.

It is difficult to specify what it might be that gives 'cause for concern' but this seems to include behaviour that would indicate that the lifer is a danger to himself or to others in the community. The lifer cannot travel abroad without permission, and is usually required to report at regular intervals to the probation office.

ALEX'S EARLY YEARS INSIDE

In all Alex spent time in 16 prisons. His initial allocation after his period on remand was to HMP Liverpool, and thereafter he was transferred to HMP Wakefield—part of the dispersal system—when he was re-classified as an adult in June 1973. From March until November 1974 he spent nine months at HMP Grendon (with its therapeutic regime), but on this occasion things did not work out, and as a consequence he was transferred to another dispersal prison—HMP Parkhurst. During all of this time he was a Category A prisoner, and his *Prison Chronicles* are largely concerned with the time that he spent at HMP Parkhurst. In all he spent just over five years there, and official reports from this time, and the patchy collection of his own writings which has survived, chronicle some of the problems that he had, and the difficulties which he encountered.

Barely 21 years old at the time of his transfer to Parkhurst, Alex later described his early years there in Granada Television's documentary *The Curious Case of Alex*, which was shown in April 1991 (see below) as '. . . struggling to stay sane. The whole thing at Parkhurst was to try and make you insane'. Indeed, Alex spent most of his time there in the Special Unit on C-wing, under the care of psychiatrists. This does not mean that Alex was psychiatrically ill. Indeed, at the time Special Units were being developed to try and cope with the growing number of young men who were being given longer and longer sentences, and who for one reason or another could not cope with imprisonment or be held within the dispersal system. As a consequence there were Special Units at HMPs Hull and Lincoln, as well as the Special Unit on C wing at HMP Parkhurst. However, perhaps the best known Special Unit was the Barlinnie Special Unit in Glasgow, which came to prominence through the publication of its most famous ex-resident's autobiography—Jimmy Boyle's *A Sense of Freedom*. Boyle, of course, was transferred to the Barlinnie Special Unit having spent many years in several of Scotland's more traditional prisons, whereas Alex was transferred into a Special Unit as a young, and very inexperienced prisoner.

It was here that Alex was to encounter some of the most notorious prisoners in the country. Again quoting from *The Curious Case of Alex*, Alex describes some of the other prisoners on the wing—'. . . this is where I met the twins [the Kray twins] . . . IRA people [and] people who've killed other prisoners'. One such prisoner was Douglas Wakefield who had murdered his uncle, and then whilst in prison murdered a sex offender. Alex, in an effort to ingratiate himself was going down to Douglas Wakefield's cell to pay his respects, and offer him a cigarette.

> I was on my way down there to give him a cigarette because I knew that he had no tobacco, but I got side-tracked. When I eventually got to his cell, the door was shut and I looked through the spy-hole and there was a dead body on the bed, and the head was half off where he had been stabbed about 20 times. Douglas Wakefield—he just sat there smoking a cigarette that he'd obviously taken off this geeza before killing him.

Such were Alex's fellow prisoners. However, what seems to have got Alex into difficulties with the prison authorities was his developing, if immature political posturing. This would take on a variety of forms. For example, Alex and others decided to set up the League for Human Rights Observation (LHRO), which amongst other things protested that prisoners were being used to test experimental drugs. Indeed prisoners have often complained that they are controlled through the use of tranquillisers, a process known to prisoners as the 'liquid cosh'. The LHRO also compiled reports from statements made by prisoners being transferred to HMP Parkhurst from Rampton Hospital that, amongst other allegations, described the torture of prisoners being held there. Alex would often sign his letters to all and sundry with the initials LHRO after his name, and by the time that he was transferred out of HMP Parkhurst he had taken over as secretary of the LHRO. Whether or not any or all of these allegations were true is not at issue, although much of what the LHRO was disclosing is now hardly sensational. Rather, at the time, what would be of concern to the prison authorities was that the very closed and secret world of HM Prison Service in the mid-1970s was being opened up to the scrutiny of the media, and that this scrutiny was being prompted by prisoners.

Alex also seems to have applied for Russian citizenship, and he petitioned the Home Office to be allowed to 'reside as a citizen of the Soviet Union' after release. In the petition, which was withdrawn before being sent to the Home Office, but which was left on his prison file, and seems to have been written in 1977, Alex describes himself as

> . . . a dedicated Communist with an organization to control. We the Communist Activist Revolutionary League, are exactly what the title implies — extreme left activist revolutionaries. We hold a deep contempt for Capitalists and the British Fascists (the so-called National Front).

He describes this fictitious organization's aim as being

> . . . to bring to the open the truth about British Gulags. We do not cause trouble, just amass facts — notably contravention's of Articles 3 and 8 and 9 of the Convention for the Protection of Human Rights . . . nothing wrong in that is there. Of course not. For if we believe that Prison Officers are also getting the rough end of the stick, then that too will be reported.

All of this is clearly the immature and overblown musings of a 24 year old idealist, and not very far removed from what one might have found on any undergraduate campus in Britain in the mid-1970s. Two years later Alex has graduated—and sounding more confident he constructs an 'Open Letter to the British Left—Disunity and Confusion', in which he appeals for the various, disunited factions of the British left to unite, and construct a Socialist Britain. Alex berates these factions for their failure to take responsibility, and act in co-ordination, for the 'problems faced by the Left in this country are more than merely considerable—they are enormous':

> In no other country can there be found a society so completely brainwashed by a capitalist order than here in Britain. In no other country is the working class so lethargically indifferent to who governs them than here in Britain. There are, admittedly, sections of the Workers that we have fighting alongside the Cause, who are the true, fully enlightened Socialists—but these sections add up to a pathetically tiny segment of the Working Class as a whole. And this state of things becomes gradually worse at every Socialist defeat—at every Capitalist victory. In the war between the Workers and their exploiters the former retain their sense of injustice—but it is only that— a sense, no more; they will not take up arms to put it right, whilst the latter retain the state, the armed services, the police, schools, newspapers, media, prisons and the prejudicial arm of the Law.

I have been unable to ascertain how the letter was to be distributed, or what impact Alex hoped that it would have had. However, in tone it certainly matched the growing militant mood of some in late-1970s Britain, and indeed Alex was in regular correspondence with at least one left wing Labour MP—Doug Hoyle. This militant mood was to become increasingly out of step with the direction that the country was to take with the election of Margaret Thatcher and her Conservative government in 1979. This is no small matter, for Mrs Thatcher's victory ushered into power a political 'World View' which had fundamental consequences for the 'politics of law and order' generally, and HM Prison Service specifically. Not only would political and financial support be given to the agencies of the criminal justice system, but also just as importantly a new mood of scepticism and disbelief became accepted in relation to the causes of crime. The fault lay not with 'society'—and, indeed, Mrs Thatcher doubted whether or not this actually existed—for creating poverty or unemployment, but within the personal make up of the offender. That's where the responsibility for any wrongdoing lay, and therefore for the 'Iron Lady', punishment of the offender made perfect popular and political sense. The sobriquet 'Iron Lady' should also remind us that Mrs Thatcher made her reputation by being tough on Communism and Communists.

The realities of this political World View had an almost immediate impact on HM Prison Service. I have already drawn attention to the changes regarding life sentences introduced by Leon Brittan whilst he was Home Secretary in 1983. However, perhaps the best known Tory initiative of these early years, neatly symbolising their political philosophy and the part that HM Prison Service was to play within that philosophy, was the regime introduced into detention centres for young offenders known as the 'short, sharp, shock'. With only slight overstatement, all the basic elements of what the Conservatives believed about the causes of crime, and how a government should respond can be seen within this regime. Criminals, especially young criminals, were not to be fussed over and helped, but rather punished, and made an example of—so that others might be deterred from thinking about crime themselves. The fact that this type of regime actually did very little to cut down on crime, and that the young offenders themselves rather enjoyed the experience, meant that within a few years the short, sharp, shock was quietly dropped. However, this would not be the last occasion that HM Prison Service would be asked to shoehorn a fundamentally political answer onto questions of criminal justice.

It would be wrong to give the impression that Alex's time at HMP Parkhurst was merely dominated by his growing political awareness. He clearly was also growing up, and in doing so developing friendships. These in turn show the side of Alex that is sensitive to the needs of others—his kindness, and desire to help. In an article written for *The Guardian*, for example, and published in January 1991, Alex recalls a death in HMP Parkhurst.

> During my first year at Parkhurst I became fairly friendly with a guy on C-wing called Andy. He came from a small place on the outskirts of Whalley, a little town in Lancashire not very far from Burnley and Nelson, where I was brought up myself. This formed the basis of our friendship. We spoke the same language . . . Andy had apparently married a foreign girl who had worked as an air hostess. He loved her very much and counted himself extremely fortunate to have found her. They had a child together and the future seemed to be very optimistic. But, after a while, Andy said, his wife turned against him and threatened to leave, taking the child with her. Andy found himself unable to bear the prospect. He killed the child and was sentenced to life . . . I must have been the first person or, rather, the first prisoner at Parkhurst whom he trusted enough to tell his story. Child killers are not well tolerated in prison generally. I believe that he was dreading the knowledge becoming known; there were some very heavy cons on the wing who would certainly have done him harm.

Word eventually gets out as to what Andy has done, and he is attacked in the prison library. According to Alex the attack was a 'severe beating', which meant that Andy had to be transferred to F2—F-wing, Hospital, second landing. Alex continues the story:

Of all the wings and landings at Parkhurst, F2 was the most feared. To be moved there was virtually to be isolated from the rest of the prison and put more directly into the hands of the psychiatrist. Usually it meant being given heavy doses of drugs and the general atmosphere itself was mindless and apathetic. I spent some time there next door to a man who believed he was an owl, and used to walk around the exercise area with a guy who spent a religious ten minutes chatting to the goldfish, throwing them dog ends to roll cigarettes with.

Alex did not meet up again with Andy until he had been transferred to HMP Grendon. By then Andy was acutely psychiatrically ill. One day, as Alex is on his way to work in the prison Andy spots him out of his window, and they share a few pleasantries:

"Alex touch that tree for me". There were some small trees growing at intervals along the front of the building. The sun was blazing down, and the leaves on the trees and the grass were green. I reached out and touched one of the trees for him. I could only stay briefly as I wasn't supposed to be there, so I gave him a wave . . . A few days later he spotted me walking by as he was cleaning his window, and shouted a greeting. This time he didn't seem as easy within himself, and just as I was about to go on my way he said, with an immeasurable sadness, and with each word drawn out: "I want someone to hold".

Andy later attacked a member of staff, resulting in him being transferred out of HMP Grendon, and back to the place that he dreaded most—HMP Parkhurst, where he cut his throat. Alex ends his story by commenting: 'I hope that I'll be able to touch a Hell of a lot of trees for him'.

AFTER PARKHURST AND 'RULE 43'

Alex himself left HMP Parkhurst in January 1980, and was downgraded to Category B. As such he moved to HMP Gartree in Leicestershire. However between January 1980 and August 1988, when he moved to HMP Grendon for the second occasion, he found it difficult to settle in any one place. In all between 1980 and 1988 Alex spent time in eight prisons: HMPs Gartree (January 1980-April 1981); Maidstone (April 1981-November 1981); Lewes (December 1981-February 1983); Blundeston (March 1983-August 1983); Bristol (September 1983-July 1985); Preston (August 1985-January 1987); Stocken (February 1987-March 1987); Lincoln (April 1987-July1988); and, Grendon (August 1988-November 1990). After his time at HMP Grendon, Alex was downgraded to Category D, and sent to HMP Leyhill, where he lasted three weeks before he absconded. As such he was 'unlawfully at large' (UAL) between December 1990 and February 1991, before handing himself in back at HMP Grendon (see below). Thereafter he was transferred to HMP Acklington as a Category C prisoner, and finally to HMP Littlehey in June 1991, from where he was eventually released in July 1993.

Various reasons are given in a number of documents as to why Alex was moved from one prison to another. However two core themes seem to emerge from the available documentation as to why he was transferred so often. Firstly, Alex does not always settle well into the differing prison regimes, and unlike his time at HMP Parkhurst he finds it difficult to make friends. For example, he claimed that he needed to be moved out of HMP Maidstone because he was being threatened by a group of prisoners, and thereafter had to be moved out of HMP Lewes for similar reasons. There has to be an element of truth in these allegations given that he sought protection under Prison Rule 43, which allowed him to be segregated from the remainder of the prison. Given that Rule 43 is often sought by sex offenders, who are at the very bottom of the prison hierarchy, Alex must have been in grave difficulties to have decided on this particular course of action. Indeed, he requested Rule 43 again whilst he was at HMP Lincoln. However, of note, it was whilst he was at HMP Stocken that he made friends with Kevin Fegan, the prison's writer-in-residence, and who was to eventually write a play about Alex's situation called *Rule 43*.

Prior to the play being performed by the Cracked Actors Theatre Company in Manchester, Fegan described the philosophical premise of the play.

> I believe that people by nature are not aggressive. They are not happy hurting other people. They get pissed, they work too hard, they take drugs. They do anything else but hurt other people. They don't get off on abusing people, so they abuse themselves.

Fegan also described the experience of long-term imprisonment as 'surreal', and explained that it was more important to understand what is happening inside a long-term prisoner's head than what he was doing with his body. He then outlined why the play was dedicated to Alex, and explained that while the play used aspects of his case it was not his life story, but rather an attempt to understand the motivation of someone who asks to be secluded from his fellow inmates. In doing so Fegan explained that prison 'offers you a good chance to confront all the existential questions. Who am I? What am I? What's it all about? But at the 15 year mark you reach a critical point. You either resign yourself to becoming institutionalised or you go berserk'.

The second theme to emerge was Alex's growing anxiety about his release from prison. This is hardly unusual, and surely we can all sympathise with the cumulative impact of an indeterminate sentence which must increase feelings of helplessness and powerlessness. Whilst there is relatively little research on this issue, there are a few British studies which are of relevance, in particular the work of Roger Sapsford (1983), which although now dated, has many advantages over other studies in that it compares lifers at different stages of their sentence. At the start of their sentence Sapsford notes that the lifer has lost the 'whole pattern' of his life, and that as a consequence over three quarters of his sample received medical reports at the beginning of their sentence which suggested some degree of psychological disturbance. This disturbance included displaying considerable anxiety; becoming increasingly timid and withdrawn; or, indeed, becoming belligerent, tense, and prone to outbursts of temper. Lifers at the stage of their sentence that Alex was at in the mid-1980s displayed according to Sapsford four traits. These were a greater tendency to talk and think about the past; increased introversion, with less interest in social activities and outgoing behaviour, which also might account for Alex's request for Rule 43; greater dependence on routine so that they made few decisions for themselves; and, a reduction in 'future time' perspective, which in essence means that the lifer would mention events in the future very close to the present time. This latter trait could easily be misinterpreted as being 'unrealistic'—a word that regularly appears in Alex's reports from the mid-1980s.

Alex was transferred to HMP Grendon in August 1988, and was to remain there until November 1990. Because of the importance of his time there this part of his sentence is dealt with in depth in the next chapter. However despite Alex's wish, and that of several of the Grendon staff group that he should be released back into the community directly from the prison, Alex was transferred to open conditions at HMP Leyhill. He lasted there for only three weeks before he 'absconded'—technically a prisoner cannot 'escape' from an open prison, as there are no walls or bars to escape over or through. Whilst he was 'at large'—on the run—he made contact with various newspapers, especially *The Guardian*, and I have already quoted from one of the stories that he had published during this period. He also made contact with Granada Television, who subsequently made the documentary about him, already mentioned, called *The Curious Case of Alex*—and he renewed his acquaintance with Kevin Fegan. Quite apart from those things that Alex himself wrote at this time, various newspaper accounts of his case were produced, including material by John Merritt in *The Observer*, Robin Thornber (below), and David Utting in *The*

Guardian. I contributed anonymously to the piece by David Utting by providing background information. In publicising the showing of *The Curious Case of Alex* one listings magazine described Alex's situation as 'Kafkaesque', and John Merritt in *The Observer* titled his piece 'Burglar Jailed for Life May be Victim of Spy Hunt Gaffe'.

It is also quite clear that Alex's friends were doing everything in their power to help him, whilst at the same time recognising that he would have to eventually return to prison to finish his sentence. Robin Thornber, for example, wrote from *The Guardian* to Sir Joseph Cantley via The Travellers Club in Pall Mall to see what the trial judge could remember of the case, and in particular whether or not he had intended Alex to remain in prison for so long. Sir Joseph's reply not particularly forthcoming. The judge did not remember 'the case of Alexandrowicz', and did not recall being told that Alex's confession had been extracted under duress. However, rather contradicting this blunt memory lapse, Sir Joseph then commented that he believed that Alex had 'a bad record . . . he had been in approved schools, borstals and prison . . . he was a public nuisance and a dangerous one'. The judge then went on to outline his reasoning behind his award of an indeterminate sentence.

> I hope that you stop "wondering" whether 20 years inside was my intention. I did not know how long he would be detained. That is why I gave him an indeterminate sentence. If I had intended him to be detained for 20 years I would have said so and that might have done him an injustice if those in charge of him thought him fit for release before that. The sentence I gave left those in charge of him to release him whenever they thought it right to do so.

This does not seem to get us very far, especially as 'those in charge' of him, as will be explained in the next chapter had been supporting Alex's release for some time.

The producers of *The Curious Case of Alex* also tried to contact the Masterson family whose house had been broken into some 20 years previously, seemingly by pushing a letter under their door. This merely prompted a solicitor's letter advising Granada Television that this approach had 'caused great distress and upset to Mrs Masterson and other members of the family who, after such a long period, do not wish to be reminded of the criminal violence which occurred'. As a result the family refused to take part in the programme, although they did suggest through their solicitor that if the producers of the programme came up with new evidence that satisfied the Home Secretary then they would reconsider their position.

It was Kevin Fegan who accompanied Alex back to HMP Grendon in February 1991, and Julia Morgan and myself who met him at the prison gate. Fegan wrote to *The Guardian* in April 1991 describing what had taken place on that day, and what had happened to Alex thereafter.

> The distressing task of returning Alex to prison fell to me. Within hours of handing him over to Grendon I received a telephone call from him at Aylesbury police station where he was kept overnight. The Home Office had obviously decided in advance that his request to remain at Grendon was not to be granted. Two days later I received a brief call from him at Oxford Prison. It was like conversing with an astronaut, he sounded so lost in time and space. I felt as though I had betrayed him. His return to prison was an extraordinary display of dignity and strength of character . . . At Oxford Prison, the adjudication tribunal[2] fined Alex £2 for absconding from Leyhill. This reinforces the attitude of the prison authorities in direct contact with him, so clearly illustrated by his last Parole Board recommendation that he should be released immediately with a six-month phase-out. Alex has now been moved to Acklington Prison in Northumberland, as far as possible from his friends in London, the Midlands and the North West. They are clearly throwing away the key. Alex cannot be expected to survive.

Fegan did not let matters end there. From his home in Stalybridge he started up a support group for Alex, called 'Free Alex Now'—'An independent public campaign for the release of Anthony Alexandrowicz—prisoner 789959'. Citing materials from *The Curious Case of Alex*, and various newspaper accounts, publicity for the support group urged people to help by raising Alex's case with their MP, and 'insisting that he or she in turn discusses the case with the Home Secretary', and writing personally to the Home Secretary. Potential correspondents were advised to mention that Alex had served 20 years, and told to expect another five years; that he was the only person since the war to be given a double life sentence for the offences which he is alleged to have committed; that there had been no answer to the allegation that a secret file exists containing a recommendation that Alex should serve 30 years; that psychiatric reports had been

---

[2] This is the formal process whereby offences against prison discipline are dealt with. The governor of HMP Grendon conducted Alex's adjudication, and it should be noted that at the time the governor of HMP Oxford was the former deputy governor of HMP Grendon. Indeed, this was why it was decided to send Alex to HMP Oxford, as a decision had been taken by Lifer Management Unit that Alex should not stay at Grendon. Obviously absconding from an open prison is a serious offence, and would normally be punished very severely. Thus Fegan is absolutely correct in his analysis as to why Alex was only given a £2 fine.

recommending Alex's release for the past ten years; and, that the prison authorities did not regard Alex as a risk to the public. Alex's prison number and address were also provided in the hope that people would write directly to him.

THE LHRO

Several people took up the challenge to write to Alex, and many others wrote to their MPs. As a consequence this forced the Home Office to provide information about Alex's case, which was in turn fed back to Alex. This information is illuminating not only because it reveals the 'line' to be taken by civil servants when discussing Alex, but also because much of the information was wrong, and clearly spun so as to put Alex in a bad light. For example, Angela Rumbold MP, at the time minister of state at the Home Office, wrote to one such correspondent alleging that Alex had remained in custody for so long as a result of continually assaulting staff, and attempting to escape. These allegations were later withdrawn. Indeed Alex himself, now moved from HMP Acklington to HMP Littlehey, continues to badger the Home Office about his case, bolstered by information provided by the support group and what they have discovered. From HMP Littlehey he also re-establishes the League of Human Rights Observance (LHRO), which had originally been set up in HMP Parkhurst. A press release written by Alex during his time at Littlehey about the LHRO exists, although there is no evidence as to whether or not this was in fact released to the press. This is an interesting document, dated 13 April 1992, as it demonstrates how far Alex had by this time matured in his understanding of how to make his case, and in relation to the various evidence he could cite in support of his views. It also provides some background as to why the LHRO had been disbanded in 1981. He alleges that the LHRO had been disbanded

> . . . because the Home Office threatened to make its members serve longer in prison if it wasn't wound up. The LHRO had just had published *The Liquid Cosh*, which had heavily criticised prison doctors for using psychotropic drugs on prisoners for purposes of "control".

Alex was to 're-form and restructure' the LHRO, according to the press release, as a consequence of the publicity surrounding the release of Stefan Kiszko, which had drawn attention to the reality of miscarriages of justice, and—unlike the original LHRO—people outside of prisons were to be allowed to join. Alex then goes on to describe the prisoners he encountered at HMP Littlehey whom he believed to be innocent.

> There are two men on the wing who have clearly been framed. They are both serving determinate sentences of nine and eleven years respectively. Unfortunately for them they are simple people who come from relatively poor homes and this means that they have no way of financing investigative journalists or solicitors or private detectives to establish their innocence. When I talk to them I feel tremendous pain for the ordeal they are being made to undergo. Both are married and have children who are growing up without a father and the likelihood is that both marriages will fold.

This passage is revealing in several respects. Firstly, it suggests Alex's understanding of the process which someone who is innocent of a crime, but who has been convicted, has to undergo and this is a theme that will be taken up in the next chapter. Secondly, it reinforces his consistent concern for the plight of others. Finally it provides a measure of how far Alex himself had come since the days when he would petition the Home Office about his release. Far from now looking to the Establishment to right the wrongs that had been done to him, he would now look outside of that Establishment for the solutions. The press release went further in this thinking, and saw the need to fundamentally re-structure the very nature of the criminal justice system itself.

> The LHRO does not accept that the system is properly just. That outside influence, especially in the Home Office and its affiliated politicians and civil servants has too much influence upon the workings of natural justice — to its detriment. Evidently so. It is my own personal opinion that the recent trickle and the coming spate of miscarriages of justice could have been prevented by the Home Office in a positive way many years ago by the simple expedient of creating an ombudsman to deal exclusively with claims of judicial miscarriage. By refusing to do that, and by instead ridiculing such claims and covering them up, by actually threatening people who protest their innocence with more captivity if they don't shut up is inexcusable. In essence, such an attitude is manifestly totalitarian, and has no legal or moral validity within Isles such as ours. Ministers have a duty to protect the public. Within that brief and inherent within that duty is that every measure must be taken to ensure that members of the public are not put into captivity by mistake . . . the LHRO stands solidly against the interference of politicians with the judicial process. They have no right to interfere because justice *must* be kept separate from politics. Once politics is allowed to interfere with justice, justice becomes hamstrung, and by definition an extension of politics, making the working of justice a political activity.

The press release ends by outlining what it is that the LHRO stands for, and will campaign on. Firstly, it wants the release from prison of all victims of judicial miscarriage; secondly, the abolition of the life sentence for anything other than murder; thirdly, the total removal of political interference from the judicial and penal processes; and finally 'removal of the Official Secrets Act from prisons so that civil servants working within them are able to freely address the public forum on any subject or matter arising from their sphere of activity'. Clearly all of these recommendations would fundamentally affect Alex's own position. However, the forces which created the circumstances for his release came not from the efforts of the LHRO, or indeed as a result of a change of heart by the Home Office, but instead from the consequences of European law on the workings of our own legal system.

CHAPTER TWO

Innocence and HMP Grendon

On 27 November 1997 more than 60 prisoners at HMPs Frankland, Long Lartin, Durham, Gartree and Maidstone went on hunger strike to highlight the number of alleged miscarriage of justice cases within the criminal justice system (CJS). The hunger strike was organized jointly by Action Against Injustice, who state that they are fighting against 'corruption in the police and legal system', and by Birmingham Prisoners Solidarity. In a flyer advertising their protest, the two groups stated that they wanted to 'have a big effect in highlighting individual campaigns [of innocence] and the level of corruption in the police and justice system today, and also build solidarity among campaigns'. The day of protest ended with a march to the offices of the Criminal Cases Review Commission (CCRC)—see *Chapter 3*—which is an independent body set up under the Criminal Appeal Act 1995 to investigate suspected miscarriages of justice.

Neither the march, nor the hunger strike by prisoners—including Winston Silcott, who having been cleared of the murder of PC Keith Blakelock, is now serving life for another murder which he claims was self-defence—attracted much media attention. Nor did it spur HM Prison Service into taking action about the philosophical possibility, and actual reality, of some prisoners being innocent after conviction. Nonetheless a series of prominent miscarriage cases, beginning with the Guildford Four who were wrongly convicted of IRA pub bombings in Guildford and Woolwich, and thereafter the Maguire Seven, Judith Ward and the Birmingham Six remind us that many people are in fact innocent of the crimes for which they have been convicted. These cases all relate to the terrorist campaigns of the IRA on mainland Britain, but a miscarriage case can have its roots in more mundane circumstances. The West Midlands Serious Crime Squad, for example, which was disbanded in 1989, under pressure to get results resorted to tactics which had hitherto seemed more common in the dictatorships of the Third and Fourth Worlds. Derek Treadaway, for example, 'confessed' to four bank robberies for which he received a sentence of 15 years. It later transpired that his 'confession' had only been extracted with the help of a series of plastic bags which had been placed over his head by policemen working within the Serious Crime Squad. Treadaway was awarded £50,000 damages in 1994. Other miscarriage cases from different police areas would include those who were alleged to have murdered the paper boy Carl Bridgewater, and Michelle and Lisa

Taylor, who were wrongly convicted of murdering the wife of Michelle's lover.

It is difficult to establish a definitive number of prisoners who are alleging to be wrongly convicted at any one time. Nor is it easy to establish how many of those who allege to be innocent are in fact eventually proven to be innocent of the crime for which they were convicted, or have had their conviction quashed. However the CCRC has estimated that at present there are over 1,000 prisoners alleging to be the victim of a miscarriage of justice, and publicised the fact that they receive new cases at the rate of five per day. The figures produced by the CCRC would seem to be confirmed by other estimates produced in 1989 by JUSTICE and the Prison Officers Association (who estimated in 1992 that there might be as many as 700 people in prison who were innocent after conviction). All of this suggests that there is likely to be a substantial proportion of the prison population innocent of the crime for which they have been convicted—and that these prisoners are likely to be concentrated within the long-term prison population.

INNOCENCE AFTER CONVICTION

Whatever number is eventually estimated, that estimate is likely to be on the low side, for there are many disincentives for prisoners, especially long-term prisoners, in maintaining their innocence. Such issues as parole, transfer, incentives, re-categorisation might all depend on the willingness of the prisoner to 'acknowledge' his guilt. So much so that the former Home Affairs specialist at *The Observer*, David Rose commented that

> For life sentenced prisoners, protesting innocence is a sure-fire way to remain in gaol forever. The inmate will be accused of having failed to "address his offending behaviour", so making it impossible to assess his future risk to the public.[3]

A miscarriage case can be seen as having three inter-related elements. Firstly, one in which an individual or individuals are treated by the state in a way which breaches their rights. Secondly, where someone is treated adversely by the state in that the punishment is disproportionate to the aim of protecting the rights of others, and

---

[3] David Rose (1996), *In the Name of the Law: The Collapse of Criminal Justice*. London: Vintage, p.34. I have written about innocence in prison in a variety of places: most recently in Eric Cullen and Tim Newell (1999), *Murderers and Life Imprisonment*, Winchester: Waterside Press

finally where the rights of others are not properly vindicated or protected by state action. All of this is of relevance to Alex's case, especially in relation to the second of the three elements, but imprisoning anyone who is innocent of a crime clearly is a miscarriage of justice. Some will argue that there are those who are 'truly' innocent, and who should be accorded a special status, as opposed to those who are innocent by way of a legal 'technicality'. However this seems specious, and we have to acknowledge that anyone who is convicted on the basis of evidence which is in fact inadmissible, or which is not proven beyond reasonable doubt should be seen as having been the victim of a miscarriage of justice. Alex himself has always denied his involvement, but there is sound reason why the conviction should not stand quite iirrespective of this. In a sense there are two miscarriages— his wrongful conviction, and the inordinate length of time for which he was held.

Some measure of the toll that maintaining their innocence inside can have on a prisoner can be gauged by the testimonies of some of those who have now been released. Vincent Hickey, for example, who together with his cousin Michael, Jimmy Robinson, and the late Pat Malloy were wrongly convicted of the murder of Carl Bridgewater, gives a flavour of how those claiming to be innocent are treated in prison. Having been released in February 1997 after spending 18 years in goal, he wrote in *The Observer* '. . . they pulled every stroke in the book to keep us in prison. They lied and lied'. He also alleges

> I am still haunted by the flashbacks. In the middle of the night my cell door used to fly open and drunken screws would burst in and beat me. Then they pissed on me. I'd be fast asleep, the next thing that I know my face has hit the floor. Now every night when I go to bed I lie down and I see it all over again. I can't sleep. The thing that gets me most is the fact that they pissed on me. The lack of dignity. In the day I can sometimes forget. It's the nights that it gets bad, and it doesn't leave me.

Innocence and HM Prison Service

Why should HM Prison Service care if the prisoners it houses are guilty or innocent? At one level some prison staff might argue that as this is an issue which is determined elsewhere within the CJS, as are appeals against conviction, that the Prison Service does not have any reason to get involved with issues related to miscarriages of justice, and more broadly with innocence. Similarly some prisoners will declare themselves innocent despite the fact that they are guilty in the hope, for example, of protecting their family, or more simply because they are 'in denial'. However, these views are at best short sighted, especially as in the long run they contribute to the general undermining of confidence that the public should have with our CJS. More specifically prisons have adopted measures that require prisoners to 'acknowledge' their guilt in order to gain parole, or improvements in regime conditions, and this adversely affects those who are innocent of the crime for which they have been convicted. At a more basic level managing prisoners who maintain their innocence is not always easy, as they often refuse to accept the reality of prison life, and if they are able to generate media interest in their campaign which in turn will create a great deal of work for the prison.

Vincent and Michael Hickey, for example, took their protestations of innocence onto the roof of HMP Long Lartin—one of the country's dispersal prison—between 26 February and 20 March 1983. The 22 days that they spent on the prison's roof compares poorly with the 89 days that Michael spent on the roof at HMP Gartree, between 24 November 1983 and 21 February 1984, and where Alex himself spent some 15 months between 1980 and 1981. Michael's feat was truly astonishing, and this in turn generated considerable media interest, but his protest could not have been sustained without the support of other prisoners within HMP Gartree. Clearly no matter how well prepared a prisoner is who wants to adopt this approach, sooner or later food runs out and it gets bitterly cold and lonely. However, describing the course of events, the journalist Paul Foot explains how Michael was able to sustain his protest for so long.

> He could not have survived for more than a few days without the sudden, spontaneous and almost unanimous support of the inmates of Gartree prison. Before long, all sorts of useful things started arriving on the roof. By the end of the second week Michael had amassed 100 new bin liners, and a huge assortment of coat hangers, broom handles, pillows and blankets. There was also an endless supply of radios—perhaps the most precious of all prisoners' possessions—which kept breaking down in the frost and damp, but were instantly replaced.[4]

Michael was also able to build a shelter against the weather, and given that the prison staff had decided on a strategy of 'starving him down', he proved more than adept at maintaining a stock of food. Foot writes that Michael '. . . got a hot meal almost every night', by

---

[4] P Foot (1986), *Murder at the Farm: Who Killed Carl Bridgewater?*, Harmondsworth: Penguin, p. 242. Foot's book remains the standard text about the Bridgewater case, and was published some eleven years before the Hickey's release. Subsequent quotes about Vincent and Michael Hickey are taken from this source.

adopting a covert plan with collaborators in the prison's residential units.

The plan contained an intricate code with letters and numbers that would be held out of the windows to let him know where the food parcel was coming from. After a few weeks Michael had a string with hooks hanging down to almost every window in the prison. He would then watch out for the code, and after a dummy run or two to confuse the officers, he would rush to the correct window and haul up his food.

Leaving on one side how embarrassing this must have been to the prison, especially given the strategy adopted to have him end his protest, it clearly also must have been a drain on resources in the prison. Managing roof-top protests, as with other demonstrations, demands the implementation of contingency plans which involve staff of a variety of grades working outside of their normal working roles; the co-ordination of those plans with HM Prison Service's Headquarters at Cleland House in London; and continued anxiety that the protest might spread, or be used as a cover for other incidents such as escapes. In the often tense culture of long-term prisons, where the balance of power between staff and prisoners is constantly being tested, having a prisoner on the roof, and being able to sustain that prisoner for over 12 weeks, must have given encouragement to many other prisoners for different protests of their own.

There are clearly better reasons for HM Prison Service to acknowledge the possibility of innocence inside than simply good prison management. For at the heart of this issue is the concept of justice, which is just as real for one prisoner as it would be for a thousand, or whatever estimate is accepted. Indeed several commentators have argued that justice should be at the heart of everything that HM Prison Service does. Lord Justice Woolf, for example, whose far-reaching report into the causes of the prison riots that swept the country in 1990, commented that,

> A recurring theme in the evidence from prisoners who may have instigated, and who were involved in the riots was that their actions were a response to the manner in which they were treated by the prison system. If what they say is true, the failure of the Prison Service to fulfil its responsibilities to act with justice created in April 1990 serious difficulties in maintaining security and control in prisons.[5]

---

[5] *Prison Disturbances April 1990 – Report of an Inquiry* (1991), London: HMSO, p.226

All of this led Woolf to conclude that there should be improved standards of justice inside—albeit, partly as a means of improving security and control—which would involve giving prisoners reasons for decisions which affected them; establishing a grievance procedure, and disciplinary proceedings to ensure that matters are reasonably dealt with; and establishing an independent complaints adjudicator. Indeed this last recommendation led to the establishment of the Prisons Ombudsman. In short Woolf raised the issue of justice in a way which both related to the actual experience of imprisonment and at the same time placed what happens in the penal system within the broader context of the CJS as a whole. So it could be argued that in much the same way that the police had to respond to the miscarriage cases through the introduction of the Police and Criminal Evidence Act 1984, and then the establishment of the Crown Prosecution Service, so HM Prison Service should be asked to develop accordingly.

Whether this view is accepted or not, what HM Prison Service currently does is to deny that there is an issue at all. Not only that, it has gone further, and actively requires prisoners to acknowledge their guilt. If they fail to do so, they worsen their position in relation to eventual release. David Rose, for example, cites the case of Andy Evans who had by 1991 manage to progress through the prison system by falsely acknowledging his guilt, and as a consequence had gained a transfer to the open prison HMP Leyhill, where Alex was also to serve some of his sentence. Despite being trusted to work in the local Gloucester community, Evans decided that he could no longer maintain his deceit in relation to the offence for which he had been sentenced, and advised the governor of the prison accordingly. That same afternoon he was transferred back to a dispersal prison.

'Throffers'—The Sex Offender Treatment Programme and Life Sentenced Prisoners

The treatment of Andy Evans comes very close to what political philosophers, such as Hillel Steiner have described as a 'throffer'— the combination of an offer or promise of a reward if a course of action is pursued, with a threat or penalty if this course of action is refused. This is obviously an exercise of power by HM Prison Service. The choice structure offers incentives to the prisoner to follow the course of action desired by the prison, making that 'choice' appear rational. It is of course rare for prison policy or regulations to be presented, or openly described in these ways, although glimpses of 'throffers' occasionally come to the surface. However, the guidance given to staff in how they should treat lifers, and the Sex Offender Treatment Programme (SOTP) offer clear examples of 'throffers' in action.

The SOTP was introduced into HM Prison Service in the early 1990s. Building on the cognitive behavioural programmes developed in Canada, the SOTP seemed to promise much in the face of growing media and moral panics about sex offenders in the community. Indeed the number of sex offenders in prison more than doubled between 1981 and 1988, when 2,692 prisoners were incarcerated with a sexual offence as their main index offence, and this number has continued to grow in the 1990s. The basis of the SOTP was explained in almost breathless terms by Eddie Guy, the civil servant in charge of DIP2, which at the time was the division of HM Prison Service that had responsibility for 'programmes for problem behaviour'. He described the four main features of the programme as housing sex offenders in fewer prisons; priority for treatment would be given to those who were likely to represent the greatest risk to the community; prisoners would be assessed following conviction as to those in most need of treatment; and, '. . . treatment programmes will be based on admission of offences, challenging attitudes, and tackling offending behaviour'.[6]

There are two main programmes within the SOTP, both of which are offence specific—the 'extended programme' for those who represent the greatest risk to the public, and the 'core programme', which requires less specialist resources. Of note, and again quoting from the article by Guy already cited, the core programme 'will tackle offenders' distorted beliefs about relationships, enhance their awareness of the effect of sexual offences on the victim, and seek to get prisoners to take responsibility for, and face up to the consequences of their own offending behaviour'. This is of course all well and good, unless of course you actually did not commit the sexual offence for which you had been convicted. Indeed it becomes even more difficult for the sexual offender who just happens to be innocent, for as Guy advises us, sex offenders are particularly prone to 'cognitive distortions', which allow them to 'rationalise' their offending. Thus protestations of innocence are merely seen as 'delusions'—the by-product of these cognitive distortions.

In relation to the 'throffer', the offer is the treatment with its promise of release, and the threat is the failure to secure release. This threat is made quite explicit, despite the fact that the SOTP wants volunteers to engage in the programme, and Guy advises us that the programme will prioritise those prisoners with the longest sentence, as this reflects the seriousness of the offence. As a consequence, 'such offenders will be subject to a selective system of parole . . . the extent to

---

6 E Guy (1992), 'The Prison Service's Strategy', in *The Penal Response to Sex Offending*, London: Prison Reform Trust, pp.1-7

which their offending behaviour has been addressed in prison is likely to be an important factor in reaching that parole decision'.

At the time all of this was being implemented one such 'sex offender' at HMP Grendon was Stefan Kiszko. Stefan spent 16 years in prison wrongly convicted of the sexual murder, in October 1975, of the schoolgirl Lesley Molseed. When he was arrested in December of that year there was no forensic evidence to link Stefan with Lesley's death. Rather he was a simple, overweight tax clerk from Rochdale, who had never been in trouble with the police, and in whom he had absolute confidence. As he went to the police station on Christmas Eve 1975 he believed that any police investigation would exonerate him, but after two days in police custody Stefan signed a 'confession' to the murder, which he subsequently withdrew. It took 16 years for Stefan to be released, and only after his solicitor discovered that he had a zero sperm count, and that tests on his semen, and semen found on Lelsley's body were incompatible—a fact that the police were aware of at the time. Stefan's biographers describe the toll of his years of wrongful incarceration.

> Was it the very fact of Kiszko's incarceration that had rendered him 'quite mad', or was it the fact that he was never regarded as a likely candidate for parole, notwithstanding that he had served longer than other convicted murderers who were released after a much shorter period of time inside. Was it his immovable belief in his own innocence . . . or was it merely the failure of any other person to consider that he might be telling the truth when he declared his innocence? Was it the persistence of those who sought to persuade him to admit his crime or was it simply an inevitable consequence of an underdeveloped and fragile personality dealt the most enormous wrong by a system of justice in which he placed so much faith?[7]

Alex did not meet Stefan at HMP Gendon, but he was clearly aware of the case. Indeed he writes an 'open letter' to the Home Office in February 1992, again explaining his own innocence, and describing what had happened whilst he was 'at large' from HMP Leyhill. In this letter he quotes Stefan's case in an effort to explain the 'pressure and threats that can be brought to bear by the police' to force a suspect to confess. Nor was Alex a sex offender. However he was a lifer, and 'throffers' can best be seen at work in the way that HM Prison Service deals with life sentenced prisoners.

---

[7] J Rose, S Panter, T Wilkinson (1997), *Innocents: How Justice Failed Stefan Kiszko and Lesley Molseed*, London: Fourth Estate, p.244

The formal source document about how life sentenced prisoners should be managed is the *Lifer Manual* (LM) of HM Prison Service.[8] It reports that lifers who maintain their innocence are 'undeniably difficult' to manage, and goes on to suggest that as a strategy for dealing with this difficulty 'it might not be helpful to get involved with discussions about guilt or innocence'. This is underscored by the fact that it makes i t clear that 'the Prison Service must take as its starting point the assumption that the prisoner was rightly convicted'. Given this position it provides advice to staff about the information required on life sentenced prisoners when they are to be considered for parole, or re-categorisation to a lower security category. It states that any reports 'must concentrate on the degree to which the lifer has addressed his or her offending behaviour', and as such outlines some of the criteria to be included in the report. This would include 'attitude to the offence':

> Does the prisoner deny guilt?
> Has the prisoner come to terms with his or her part in the offence, and accepted responsibility for it?
> Is he or she ready to talk about it?
> Assess the prisoner's attitude towards others who may have been involved, and the victim.
> State the degree of remorse, if any expressed.

This is the reality of the life sentenced prisoner, and the culture of HM Prison Service in its outlook to those prisoners who maintain their innocence. It was also a reality that Alex would have to deal with when he was transferred to HMP Grendon in the summer of 1988.

HMP GRENDON

HMP Grendon opened in 1963, just two years prior to the abolition of capital punishment. This background is significant as it suggests something of the growing social change being experienced by the country in a period which also saw homosexuality legalised, the Open University founded, an Equal Pay Act established, and the implementation of race relations legislation. Old beliefs were being challenged, and there was an air of optimism and progress. The first governor and medical superintendent of the prison, Dr William Gray, caught something of the atmosphere when he wrote that HMP Grendon

---

[8] All quotes taken from *Lifer Manual: A Guide for Members of the Prison and Probation Services Working with Life Sentenced Prisoners*, H M Prison Service, 1996. A copy of the manual is available at the offices of the Prison Reform Trust.

was 'a unique establishment . . . attempt[ing] for the first time, in an English prison, a therapeutic approach to the psychiatric treatment of non-psychotic recidivist offenders with moderate to severe personality disorders'.[9] From the outset the Grendon regime contained the four basic elements of the classic therapeutic community: a democratic exercise of power over the administrative and therapeutic life of the prison: permissiveness in relation to previous and ongoing behaviours, thus allowing those behaviours to be acknowledged or worked through; confrontation and presentation of those behaviours so as to reveal how they affect others within the prison; and, communalism, through the establishment of close interactive relationships.

A simple description of the regime of the prison at the time that Alex was there reveals glaring differences between life at Grendon, and that of any other Category B prison. Staff and inmates are on first name terms, and the daily work of the prison revolves around groups. Prisoners are unlocked at 0745 hours each morning and remain unlocked until 2100 at night. Each wing houses 40 prisoners and each prisoner is assigned to a group of seven other prisoners. This group is led by a member of staff who might be a prison officer, a psychiatrist, a psychologist, or someone from the education or probation departments. Each group has a broad mix of offenders so as to ensure that armed robbers mix with sex offenders, that arsonists mix with murderers, or that burglars mix with paedophiles. Thus the traditional 'nick hierarchy' which sees notorious armed robbers—'blaggers'—and murderers at the top, and sex offenders—'nonces'—at the bottom, subject to the constant threat of abuse necessitating their segregation from other prisoners on rule 43 is totally absent. A strict 'no violence' rule initiated and upheld by the prisoners themselves has facilitated the communalism which is at the heart of the therapeutic community, and stands in stark contrast to the attacks on sex offenders which are common in other penal environments. What is shared in these small groups of eight prisoners is fed back into the wing group, when all 40 inmates and staff share what has been discussed. There are no secrets at Grendon, or as Gray put it, 'no Prisoners' Code', and many inmates find this hard to accept, often describing their time at the prison as the hardest 'bird' that they have had to serve.

Inmates on the prison's therapy wings develop and maintain their own prohibitive rules against violence, sex, and drug taking, and those who transgress these rules are 'voted out' of the prison by the wing

---

9 W J Gray (1973), 'The English Prison Medical Service', in G Wolstenholme, M O'Connor (Eds.), *The Medical Care of Prisoners and Detainees*, Amsterdam: Elsevier

communities and returned to their sending establishment—known universally at Grendon as 'the system'. There is no punishment or segregation block, and some measure of the motivation to abide by these rules can be gauged by the fact that in comparison with other prisons Grendon has consistently had the lowest number of offences recorded against prison discipline. This is no small achievement given that the vast majority of prisoners come to Grendon because of their violent behaviour. Since its origin in 1963 there has been only one escape, one major hostage incident, but no riots or rooftop demonstrations. Prisoners vote for a wing 'chairman' or 'cabinet', and food and television 'reps', as well as electing members of various administrative committees within the prison. Assaults on staff are virtually non-existent, and 'socials' to which members of the public are invited are held regularly.

This was the environment that Alex came into contact with when he was transferred to the prison in August 1988. After a period of assessment he was located on D wing, where the wing therapist was the head of the prison's Psychology Department, Dr Eric Cullen. Alex was fortunate in this allocation, for in Cullen he found a passionate advocate of his case, and someone who was to become a life-long friend. This was often no easy matter, for as Eric began to unravel the circumstances of Alex's offence, and especially the length of time he had served, he risked a great deal to raise this matter time after time not only within Grendon itself, but also externally with Home Office ministers and the Home Secretary himself. Indeed events would eventually come to a head when Eric took on David Mellor MP, the then minister of state at the Home Office, about Alex's case, and a senior member of the current Prison's Board was dispatched to Grendon to remind Eric that he was 'either an "Action Group" or a civil servant', asked to choose, and then given a formal verbal reprimand about his behaviour.

As the wing therapist Eric was responsible for the physical and mental wellbeing of the residents of the wing, and it was his role to co-ordinate the therapeutic programme that they undertook. Eric remembers that when he first met Alex he was 'withdrawn, guarded and surly—he was very defensive'. I put it to him that most Grendon prisoners are like this, especially at the start of their therapy, but Eric felt that Alex was much more so, describing him as having a 'fortress mentality'. Ten years later Eric describes for me Alex at the start of this therapy,

Alex had been devastated by imprisonment, and that was obvious to anyone who looked at him for more than a few seconds. His health was wrecked, and actually I think that he was on the verge of becoming a nervous wreck—he was despairing. I did get close to him, but not so that my judgement was impaired. In fact it focussed my understanding of the pain that he was feeling.

Gradually Alex began to participate in the life of the wing, eventually becoming wing vice-chairman, and started to take part in therapy groups. This was no small matter, as Grendon's therapy is predicated upon the offender accepting his guilt. (Stefan Kiszko was never in therapy, but located instead in the prison's Acute Psychiatric Unit.) Given this, why was Alex accepted into Grendon at all? Eric tries to answer this question by addressing both Alex's circumstances directly, and also speaking more generally about Grendon:

> Technically, Alex shouldn't have come at all, but Grendon is also about helping people come to terms with themselves, not just about coming to terms with crime. It is about helping people who have lost their lives to re-discover themselves, and thereafter re-integrate back into the World. Ultimately he was accepted because that is what Grendon is like—it is a uniquely positive place, which obliges people who have lived their lives lying, and brutalising to change that behaviour. It recruits prisoners to convert and become elders of a community, which uses collective responsibility to challenge—through honest discussion—life-long beliefs. Alex wasn't the first innocent person to be accepted at Grendon, and he won't be the last.

This passionate account of the uniqueness of Grendon is typical of those ex-staff that have worked there, and also of former prisoners who have gone through its therapy. Mark Leech, for example, in his powerful autobiography, writes,

> I arrived at Grendon Underwood at 5 pm on Thursday 11 May 1989. The atmosphere was totally different from the one I had left behind me that morning in the mists of sodden Dartmoor. Here there were pleasant gardens blooming with flowers and people with smiles on their faces. The reception, a small single-storey building close to the gate lodge, was also noticeably different. The reception procedure was over very quickly and the screws 'asked' you to wait in the waiting room, rather than barking the usual order.[10]

During his time in therapy Leech not only came to terms with his offending behaviour—so much so that he has become chairman of a new association for ex-offenders called Unlock, but also started to write

---

[10] M Leech (1992), *A Product of the System*, London: Victor Gollancz, p. 122. All subsequent quotes are taken from this source. Mark Leech is also the editor of the annual *Prisons Handbook*, Waterside Press.

award winning prose and drama. Perhaps this is why he dedicates his book to Grendon, which he describes as a 'harsh regime [for] there is no hiding away from your faults for there are 40 other people only too happy to point them out to you; they are displayed for all to see and discuss'. He continues:

> I found the changing process exceptionally difficult, but I knew without it I was destined to spend the rest of my life in one type of penal regime or another.

As Leech describes, prisoners were and remain eager to go to Grendon because the prison has an unparalleled success rate at getting very violent prisoners to turn away from crime. Rather than 'short, sharp shocking' them into a change of behaviour, the therapeutic process described by Eric Cullen and Mark Leech is almost HM Prison Service's best kept secret, because rarely does this therapeutic impulse coincide with the political fashion about what to do with offenders. Nonetheless the most recent academic study of reconviction rates at the prison,[11] which examines the reconviction rates within four years of a number of prisoners who went to HMP Grendon for therapy between 1984-1989 shows that prisoners treated there have lower reconviction rates than might have been expected if they had not gone to Grendon. Of note, the research also found that time spent at Grendon was strongly related to reconviction. In short, reconviction rates were lower for prisoners who stayed for longer periods, and prisoners who stayed 18 months at Grendon exhibited reductions in reconviction rate of around one-fifth to one-quarter. The research also suggested that 'mode of release' from the prison affected reconviction rates. In other words there was a treatment impact on whether the prisoner was released back into the community after his stay at HMP Grendon, or alternatively whether he was transferred back into 'the system' at the end of therapy.

This research is of relevance to Alex's case, especially when it comes to understanding the controversy surrounding the way he was to be released from the prison. Also whilst the description provided so far might have been acceptable to Eric, how would Alex's protestations of innocence go down with other prisoners on his therapy groups? After all, the old saying of 'you can't cheat a cheater' reveals something of how intuitive other offenders are about the sincerity of their colleagues on therapy. Eric remembers that:

---

[11] P Marshall (1997), *A Reconviction Study of HMP Grendon Therapeutic Community*, Home Office Research and Statistics Directorate, Research Findings No 53. All figures and quotes are taken from this publication.

Alex took part in the groups and was extremely popular. We interrogated him extensively in the early months about the denial of the offence. Unusually, he convinced the prisoners as to his innocence more quickly than the staff, as it is usually the other way around, and from then on he wasn't really challenged as he was believed.

Not only that, Eric also describes Alex's personal qualities as contributing to the acceptance of his innocence:

> He seemed naturally and without any design on his part to assume authority in the community. I can only put that down to his honesty, integrity, and frankly his wisdom. He was also clearly committed to non-violence, which for someone who had had to survive in the dispersal system was very impressive. Frankly it made him a poignant figure.

All of this was going to become a problem, for as Eric attests 'prisons don't like protestations of innocence—the worst thing that a prisoner can do is protest his innocence and criticise the system. Alex did both'. How did Eric account for what had happened to Alex in relation to the length of time that he had served?

> In the early years he behaved rebelliously: he assaulted someone who had raped him; he wrote to the Russian PM asking for Soviet citizenship; he started a Communist-like Party in prison; and, he associated with activists. That alone would have been enough to have kept him buried for years. A couple of doctors also wrongly labelled him 'psychopathic', which again is not going to help him get released. From 1982 onwards his outlook became more positive, and by 1985 he was being openly recommended for release. At Grendon this recommendation became a clarion call, and I was his cheerleader—his self-appointed spokesperson.

Becoming Alex's 'self-appointed spokesperson' involved buttonholing every politician who visited the prison, and advising them of Alex's circumstances. As HMP Grendon was and remains on the 'official tour' of every new minister for prisons, or Home Secretary, there were plenty of politicians for Eric to talk to. Angela Rumbold, David Mellor, and Douglas Hurd all visited the prison during Alex's time there, and Eric made sure that he raised Alex's case with them all. As has already been alluded to, this was to land Eric in trouble on more than one occasion, and he has retained a record of the correspondence that flowed between the Home Office and the prison. For obvious reasons Eric does not want these letters to be quoted, but a taste of their contents can be gauged from his own account of one of his attempts to raise Alex's case with David Mellor.

I was too vociferous that he should be released, but all the evidence—from governors, psychiatrists, members of the Board of Visitors, and so forth—gave unqualified recommendations for his release. Mellor said 'No', and then didn't bother to give an explanation. In fact no-one at the Home Office wanted to explain their position, probably because they didn't have a position to explain. But I don't regret getting too close to Alex. I'm pleased that I did, and that I had the opportunity to meet him, and challenge my own integrity. I rebuke the Home Office and the Prison Service for they were wrong, and they are still wrong.

Ironically, Alex and HMP Grendon were to face their most severe test not as a result of political interference, but from a rather more prosaic problem. In December 1989 the staff were given just 48 hours to evacuate the premises as a result of acute electrical problems that threatened to burn the place down. Most of the prisoners were evacuated to HMP The Mount in Hemel Hemsptead, where Julia Morgan and myself tried to hold the fort in the face of great pressure from The Mount's governor to have us evicted. Others, including Mark Leech, were transferred to HMP Winchester, and most of the life sentenced prisoners, including Alex, were sent to HMP Wormwood Scrubs. Several months later we were all re-united at HMP Wellingborough, which like The Mount was none too pleased to have us take over part of their prison, before Grendon was once again ready for occupation. This period in the prison's history has never been described before in any depth, but it is of great significance both for the prison, and for those prisoners who had to test their new therapeutic outlook in 'the system'.

The fear on the staff side was that the politicians would take the opportunity to close the prison down once and for all. After all the prison's therapeutic regime hardly fitted with the government's approach to crime and punishment. For the prisoners, especially those who had gone to HMPs Winchester and Wormwood Scrubs, they were concerned that they would have to live by a new code in an environment that was totally unsympathetic, and at times downright hostile. So the temptation was to return to the values and outlook that had served them well in the dispersal system, or in traditional Category B prisons. In short therapy 'was off' until Grendon re-opened.

Some prisoners certainly adopted this approach, and I remember visiting HMP Wormwood Scrubs in an attempt to keep up morale and bring news of developments about the prison, only to be greeted by clearly tripping eyes, and the caution that comes when a prisoner speaks to 'a suit'. To his credit Alex remained committed to therapy, and Eric remembers that

Alex had been elected an unofficial chairman at the Scrubs, and when I visited him I found him giving strength and support to the other lifers, encouraging them and keeping their spirits up. This was often in great contrast with some of the others who had drifted back into system ways, but not Alex.

Just months after the prison was re-opened with its new wiring system Alex was moved to HMP Leyhill in November 1990, where, as has been described, he was to abscond just a few weeks later. Ironically this abscond came just hours after Eric had visited him at the prison, which was again to get Eric into trouble. Nonetheless Eric stuck by Alex, and was to attend his Discretionary Lifer Panel at HMP Littlehey (see below) as a witness, and they have remained in contact since Alex's release. Indeed it was Eric and his wife Margaret that took Alex to lunch on the day of his release, along with Debbie a friend of Alex's. Eric remembers that Alex was

> delighted but completely bewildered. He was released within two weeks of the news [of his DLP]. And what assistance was he offered from the Prison Service? Bugger all. That's bugger all, and you can quote me.

CHAPTER THREE

The Law and Lifers, Release and the Criminal Cases Review Commission

This final chapter attempts to bring Alex's story up-to-date by describing the process of his release from prison, and what has happened to him thereafter. As such it begins by describing the law as it applies to prisons generally, and then more specifically to discretionary life sentenced prisoners. In doing so it outlines the growing influence of the European Court of Human Rights on prisons in this country, and especially the influence that European legislation had on the drafting of the Criminal Justice Act 1991. Without the influence of the European Court there is every possibility that Alex might still be incarcerated. The chapter also describes the origins and development of the Criminal Cases Review Commission (CCRC), which was set up to investigate alleged miscarriages of justice, and through which Alex is still pursuing a claim in his quest for justice. They are his last hope.

As with the previous chapters I have continued to try and give Alex a voice. In this respect I have again been helped by having access to Eric Cullen's papers. Eric attended Alex's Discretionary Lifer Panel (DLP) (see below), and kept copious notes of what he said there, and of the process itself. I have also been able to interview Eric about his memories of the day, and events thereafter. Not only that, in filming Alex for *Clear My Name* I visited him in his home in Milton Keynes, and met with him on other occasions with one of his key supporters, which has given me some insight into his fears, anxieties, and his hopes for the future. The chapter starts by looking at the law and its application in prison.

PRISON AND THE LAW

The law relating to prisoners and prison is simple and straightforward, at least in terms of legal theory. Primary legislation is contained within the Prison Act of 1952, and secondary legislation in the Prison Rules of 1984 (soon to be 1999). Similarly, when in 1972 Lord Denning, at the time Head of the Court of Appeal (Civil Division), in *Becker v Home Office* ruled that the Prison Rules did not give prisoners any rights at all, he effectively placed a block on legal challenges brought by prisoners against the prison authorities. Denning argued that if courts were to 'entertain actions by disgruntled prisoners' the governor's life would be made 'intolerable'.[12] In 1975 he went further, and ruled that prisoners had no right to be legally represented at a governor's or a Board of Visitors' adjudication, and a year later that life sentenced prisoners had no right to know why their release was refused. Denning's rulings initially set the tone for how the law and prisons would operate; in short, the two were to be as separate as oil and water. Yet even as he was deciding that prisoners had no rights whatsoever, the European Court was taking a very different view in response to its first ever British case.

Golder v UK (1975) 1 EHRR 524, Series A, No 18 ruled that prisoners who wanted to complain to their solicitors about their treatment inside did not have to be subject to 'prior ventilation'. 'Prior ventilation' was the Prison Service requirement that prisoners had to have raised a matter that they wished to complain about within the prison itself before they could raise that matter externally. The European Court ruled that this violated Article 6 of the Convention On Human Rights—the right of access to the courts. It also ruled that, as Mr Golder had been stopped by the prison from contacting his solicitor, this was itself in violation of Article 8 of the Convention—the right to respect for correspondence.

Whilst this European influence would become even more important in the years to come, the basic simplicity of the primary legislation in relation to prisons also began to prompt domestic legal challenges as this legislation was constantly having to be supplanted by other documents and instructions. These documents are now known as Prison Service Standing Orders (PSOs) and Prison Service Instructions (PSIs), and in effect provide detailed guidance to prisons on how to implement policy. As these documents offer governors a great deal of personal discretion, the courts have gradually intervened to determine the precise nature of a prisoner's rights and entitlements. These interventions can be seen on two broad fronts. Firstly, in relation to public law, where there has been legal challenge in relation, for example, to parole, transfer, and home leave entitlements; and, secondly in respect of civil law where it is alleged that prison staff have been negligent in some way.

The two landmark cases within the British courts were the decision of the Court of Appeal in 1979 in *R v Board of Visitors of Hull Prison ex parte St Germain*, and in 1983 in *Raymond v Honey* [1983] 1 AC 1. This

---

[12] There are now various accounts of the law relating to prisoners and prison. In my opinion, the best is S Livingstone and T Owen (1993), *Prison Law: Text and Materials*, Oxford: Clarendon Press. The cases cited, and any quotes used are taken from this source.

latter case arose out of a dispute when the prison governor—Colin Honey, stopped a letter from the prisoner—Mr Raymond being sent to his solicitor. The House of Lords in effect ruled that prisoners did in fact retain all their civil rights that were not expressly taken from them by Act of Parliament, such as the disenfranchisement of convicted prisoners. The St Germain case concerned a Canadian prisoner—Ronald St Germain, who challenged an adjudication by the Board of Visitors at HMP Hull following riots at that prison in 1976. The Court of Appeal ruled that there had been substantial breaches in the rules of natural justice in the way in which Mr St Germain's and other similar adjudications had been conducted, and laid down a number of guiding principles as to how adjudications should be processed in the future.

Clearly with the numbers of mandatory and discretionary lifers in our prisons it was not going to take too long before the European Court began to take an interest in their circumstances. However, given Alex's status, this brief review will only outline the major cases that transformed the circumstances of release in relation to discretionary lifers. The first case of a discretionary lifer to reach the European Court was that of Robert Weeks, who had been sentenced to life imprisonment at the age of 17 in 1966, when he pleaded guilty to an armed robbery in a pet shop in Gosport. Weeks had entered the shop with a starting pistol loaded with blanks, threatened the shopkeeper, and robbed him of 35 pence. He then telephoned the police to give himself up. When they arrived he took the starting pistol out of his pocket, and unfortunately it went off, although no one was injured. He was released on licence for the first time in 1976, but was recalled to prison a year later, and thereafter he was subsequently re-released and again re-detained several times between 1977 and 1986.

The European Court upheld Mr Weeks's claim that on his recall to prison in 1977, and at reasonable intervals throughout his detention, he had not been able to challenge that imprisonment within the requirements of Article 5(4) of the European Convention On Human Rights. This states that 'everyone who is deprived of his liberty by arrest or detention shall be entitled to take proceedings by which the lawfulness of his detention shall be decided speedily by a court and his release ordered if the detention is not lawful'.[13] The court took the view that a discretionary life sentence was not simply about punishment, but also about the protection of others, and rehabilitation of the offender. As a consequence the circumstances of the person sentenced to a

---

[13] This text is taken from Livingstone and Owen (1993) p.272, and I have relied heavily on their account of the process of the release of discretionary life sentenced prisoners.

discretionary life sentence would change over time, and it was their legal entitlement to have their case regularly reviewed by a 'court'. Significantly the Parole Board did not qualify as a court, as it only had advisory functions, and was not therefore to order a prisoner to be released if it believed that the circumstances of that prisoner's detention had become unlawful. The European Court also took into consideration the fact that a prisoner did not have access to reports considered by the Parole Board, and thus was not truly able to participate in the decision making process.

The Weeks judgement did not in itself change the procedures for reviewing the detention of discretionary lifers, but it paved the way for the second case to reach the European Court of Human Rights. Thynne, Wilson and Gunnell were three discretionary life sentenced prisoners who, unlike Weeks, had all been convicted of very serious offences. Nonetheless they also argued that their continued detention was in breach of Article 5(4), and that they were entitled to have their case reviewed by 'a court' in ways which the Parole Board could not satisfy. The European Court upheld this view, clearly drawing attention to the two distinct components of a discretionary life sentence: put simply that there was a 'tariff' element to the sentence, which was in essence the punishment for the offence that had been committed, thus meeting the requirements of deterrence and retribution; secondly, that there was a security, or 'risk' element which conferred responsibilities on the Home Secretary to determine when the prisoner was safe to release. In effect this ruling forced the government to change the process for reviewing the detention of discretionary lifers once they had completed the tariff portion of their sentence, and these changes were given authority through the Criminal Justice Act 1991.

The CJA 1991 and Discretionary Lifer Panels (DLPs)
The Criminal Justice Act 1991 reflected these decisions of the European Court by devising suitable arrangements to review the continued detention of discretionary life sentenced prisoners after their tariff period (the period deemed to be appropriate for purposes of punishment and fixed by the secretary of state after considering any recommendation by the sentencing judge) had ended. In effect from the implementation of the 1991 Act a discretionary life sentence has two distinct components related firstly to punishment, and secondly to risk. This latter component, as set out in the judgements of the European Court, is seen to change over time, and hence the need for a judicial mechanism of review. This mechanism was the Discretionary Lifer Panel (DLP). Except in exceptional circumstances these changes were extended to those sentenced before 1991, and it was calculated that at

the time there were some 330 prisoners who fell into this category. Alex was one of those prisoners, and all were to have their cases reviewed by a DLP by the end of 1993.

The chairman of the Parole Board appoints a DLP, which is made up of three members. A judge chairs each DLP—so as to satisfy the judicial element, ensuring that it has the authority of a court. A High Court judge will chair a DLP involving a prisoner convicted of a terrorist offence, serial rape, attempted murder of a policeman or prison officer, and so forth, and a circuit judge will chair all other DLPs. The other two members of the DLP might include a psychiatrist, psychologist, criminologist, or probation officer. Both the secretary of state and the prisoner may be legally represented at the DLP, and each can call witnesses. However each party must request in writing their desire to call a witness, who must also be identified, and an outline provided of the substance of the evidence that they are likely to provide. The chair of the DLP decides whether or not the witness can be called, and gives reasons in writing if a request for a witness is refused. The hearing of the DLP takes place within the prison where the prisoner is detained, and any decision taken at the hearing is communicated to the prisoner in writing within a maximum of seven days.

Of note, and certainly of relevance in Alex's case, under Section 34 (3) of the Act it is only a direction by the DLP to release a prisoner on licence that binds the Home Secretary. The test for release is that the DLP is 'satisfied that it is no longer necessary for the protection of the public that the prisoner should be confined', which satisfies the second phase of a discretionary life sentence within the rulings of the European Court.

I have had access to the various documents related to Alex's DLP, which was held on 22 June 1993 at HMP Littlehey as Eric Cullen was called as a witness. As a consequence I have a blow by blow account of the course of events on the day in question, and have been able to interview Eric at length about his recollections of the day. As far as I am aware this is the first time that any description of the course of an actual DLP has been given. Yet these documents might never have made it into any form of public record, as it is clear that the Home Office did not want Eric to be called as a witness on Alex's behalf. A note in his files about Alex exists from Judi Kemish of Birnberg and Co, who represented Alex at the DLP, requesting his attendance on the day as Eric 'will be able to give evidence re: Mr Alexandrowicz's state of mind; the element of risk and extensive insight into the whole person that Grendon prison uniquely affords'. As Eric was still head of psychology at HMP Grendon, and thus still a 'civil servant'—but one who had made his position clear about where he stood in relation to Alex's release, HM Prison Service were none to pleased at the prospect of what Eric might say. The authority for accepting or rejecting witnesses lay with the chair of the DLP. In Alex's case this was His Honour Judge David Smith QC. He wrote to the Secretary of the Parole Board early in June 1993 outlining his view about the calling of witnesses. After giving details about his own availability he comments,

> I am prepared to hear any of the witnesses that are suggested. I hope that the letter we send makes it plain that although we are prepared to hear the witnesses it is for the prisoner to arrange their attendance. In many instances the witnesses requested are presumably available at Littlehey but it is for the prison authorities to say whether they will make the witnesses available . . . Alexandrowicz wants to call Dr Cullen from Grendon. If he is willing to come *and if the authorities are prepared to let him come we shall listen to him.* That is all I am saying. We are not ordering him to come. (Emphasis added)

This ruling is, of course, open to interpretation. Despite the fact that it is for the chair of the DLP to decide who can or cannot be called as a witness, in this instance it seems that discretion is being allowed to the 'authorities'. How these 'authorities' were to decide as to Eric's attendance or otherwise is revealed in an exchange of correspondence that centres, of all things, on whether Eric was to be paid travelling expenses from HMP Grendon to HMP Littlehey! For example, a letter in Alex's file from a civil servant at the Parole Board exists pointing out that,

> The Prison Service's policy is that prison staff should attend as witnesses at Discretionary Lifer Panel hearings where directed to do so by the Parole Board. While the Prison Service would not wish to prejudice a prisoner's case in any way, attendance at hearings can be very expensive and time consuming and, in the interests of ensuring the best use of public funds, our view is that wherever possible evidence should be provided in writing by staff who are not employed at the establishment in which the prisoner concerned is located.

Of course it would have been extremely odd to have forbidden Eric to attend, and this bureaucratic hurdle related to expenses was used as a device, seemingly in an attempt to put Eric off. Thus Eric was only to be allowed to attend if the 'question of the reimbursement of any travelling expenses incurred by Dr Cullen' was resolved so that they were not paid out of public funds!

The resolution of this question did not put Eric off from attending, nor did it deter the Free Alex Now (FAN) campaign from organizing a demonstration on the day in question outside the gates of the prison. Kate Holdom, the FAN co-ordinator, wrote to other members describing the plan for the day, and giving directions to the prison.

> As you know Alex has a Parole Board hearing (sic) during the week of 22nd of June . . . Kevin Fegan, myself and other FAN supporters will be demonstrating outside Littlehey Prison on the day of Alex's hearing. Littlehey is where Alex is currently imprisoned and is also where the hearing will take place. As the judge arrives on the morning of the hearing we will present him with a large petition requesting the immediate release of Alex. Alex is very much in favour of a demonstration and obviously we need maximum participation for maximum effect.

This was clearly successful, as Eric remembers that it was a sunny day, and that there was a FAN demonstration as he entered the prison.

> There were about 15 people there, at the entrance of the prison, holding placards, and there was also some media coverage. It made me feel very positive about the day, although I did think that it might put off the panel.

Eric also remembers that whilst he had done about six DLPs by the time of Alex's hearing, that Alex's was 'unique . . . It stood out, as the atmosphere was so intense. Not only that, Judi Kemish was so obviously committed to Alex's case, and even now I feel that that made a difference'. He also recalls that 'Alex was on the verge of nuclear meltdown. He was a gibbering wreck—practically hyperventilating', which reveals something of the tension of the day. Indeed, several years later he can still remember the atmosphere in the hearing room.

> The tension was acute. There had been a prolonged tension building throughout the day, so that by the end Alex was pale and chain smoking. In fact he was a serial smoker, so much so that when everything was over he was coughing, and his voice was raw.

Eric's hand-written account of what he said on the day to the DLP still exists, and I will quote at length from this as it reveals the case for Alex's immediate release. This is of great relevance, as it became clear that the preferred Home Office option for Alex was that he should be transferred again to open conditions prior to release, which in all likelihood would have meant that he would have spent another three or four years in custody. After outlining his contact with Alex, and his own qualifications, Eric sets out the reasons why Alex should be released based on three factors—the length of time that Alex had served; questions related to risk; and other issues he describes as 'additional factors'. However, throughout his testimony Eric avoids raising the issue of Alex's innocence, as this would be a matter for another day.

> Length of sentence: Here I would make three particular points. Firstly Alex was convicted in 1971 of crimes which, in normal tariff currency would mean he would have been released between 1976 and 1984. There is no constraint on fixed sentence offenders' release from custody based on hypothetical risk. Secondly he has served over eight years beyond his official tariff date. Finally he has served significantly longer than the majority of life sentenced prisoners regardless of their crimes and I know of no other serving prisoner in the United Kingdom who has been imprisoned for so long for relatively minor crimes.

Eric then goes on to tackle the question of the risk that Alex might pose should he be released back into the community.

> The trial judge said "I am going to pass upon you a sentence which may sound very savage but it is not as savage as it may seem to you. It is a sentence which, when you are fit and the doctors are confident about you, they will put you back in society". In 1983, a Consultant Forensic Psychiatrist thought "natural justice demanded Mr Alexandrowicz's release after his long imprisonment". Every Psychiatrist since 1986 has confirmed clearly and emphatically that he is not suffering from any mental disorder and that he is safe to be released. This is also the unanimous view of [the staff of HMP Grendon]; the Grendon governor [then the most experienced governor in the Prison Service and now a member of the Parole Board]; and the Parole Board recommended granting a Provisional Release Date . . . It is therefore safe to conclude that, without reservation, everyone involved in the assessment of risk who had any direct knowledge of the prisoner concerned was completely satisfied that Alexandrowicz was safe to be released.

Of the 'additional factors' that Eric outlined to the DLP, the most important was to try and get the panel to understand why Alex had absconded from HMP Leyhill, after his transfer there from HMP Grendon. Indeed this abscond had been especially embarrassing for Eric given that Alex had disappeared only hours after Eric had visited him at Leyhill. After describing the circumstances of Alex being transferred to open conditions, despite being recommended for release from HMP Grendon, Eric pointed out that the transfer to HMP Leyhill would have nonetheless meant 'at best' release in 1993, and 'at worst' even longer. He also pointed out that there was a fallacy behind the theory that prisoners could be 'tested' in open conditions.

It is essential to understand and accept that the capacity to adjust successfully to prisons does not necessarily have any bearing on capacity to adjust to freedom. In fact, it could be cogently argued that the opposite may be true. There is absolutely no empirical evidence to indicate that time spent in a Category D prison is preferable to time spent either in a supervised hostel, Pre-Release Employment Scheme or in freedom. The staff at Grendon had provided detailed arguments for Alexandrowicz using the supportive regime of Grendon as a base from which he might progress through an integrated release programme with informed graduated responsibility. This is precisely what is now happening with dozens of our current population under the new Criminal Justice Bill to excellent effect. The Home Office's own research department had informed the House of Lords' Select Committee on Life Imprisonment that the overwhelming majority of Leyhill lifers had said that they had not needed the additional hoops to jump through which that particular regime provided.

Finally, Eric concluded that,

> I would argue that the Prison Service releases men every day who are far more likely to re-offend than Alex, lifers and non-lifers alike. They are not the subjects of interminable speculation, conjecture and scrutiny. They have none of the overwhelming affirmation afforded to Alex by literally dozens of staff: governors, psychiatrists, psychologists, probation officers, chaplains, prison officers and group managers, Board of Visitors and Parole Board members, confirming that he is safe to release *now*.

This was powerful testimony indeed. Eric also remembers that there 'were no surprises at the DLP', as a result of the 'cumulative weight of evidence' for Alex to be released. Indeed the panel only deliberated for 30-40 minutes before they decided to reject the preferred Home Office option to transfer Alex to open conditions, and grant his immediate release. Eric recalls that 'Alex was in a state of shock—he was numb. I congratulated him. My own feeling was an equal measure of excitement and relief, but also anger that it had taken so long to do justice'. Significantly he also suggests that 'I think that there comes a point when it is no longer possible to do justice. The scales had been tipped for too long'.

RELEASE AND THE CRIMINAL CASES REVIEW COMMISSION

Alex was released only weeks after the decision of the DLP, but that is not the end of his story. Not only was release merely the beginning of a new struggle for survival in the reality of living in a society that is less than welcoming to former prisoners, but also Alex had still not cleared his name. He might have been released from prison after an inordinate length of time, but he remained convicted of the crimes that had been committed in the Masterson house on the evening of the 7 October 1971. Not only that, he was now subject to the conditions of a life licence, which—as the name implies—remains in force for the rest of Alex's life; and, if he fails to abide by any of the conditions contained within the licence he can be recalled to prison.[14] Of course all of this would become academic if Alex was able to prove his innocence, and the way to do this is through the Criminal Cases Review Commission (CCRC).

The CCRC was set up by the Criminal Appeal Act 1995, but the CCRC's origins stem from a Royal Commission on Criminal Justice announced by the then Home Secretary, Kenneth Baker in March 1991. Baker was later to explain his thinking in his autobiography.

> Having dealt with several of the alleged miscarriages of justice I came to the conclusion that the system needs to be changed. Such allegations should not come to the Home Secretary for him to consider whether they should be referred to the Court of Appeal. They should instead be submitted to a separate Authority which would investigate them and examine any new evidence. That Authority should have extensive powers of investigation and examination. If it found that allegations of a miscarriage of justice were not frivolous but cast serious doubts over the soundness of a verdict, then it would refer the case either to the Court of Appeal or to a separate Court which would reopen the matter in a less formal way than the usual adversarial style of the British Courts.[15]

Given this type of reasoning the Royal Commission's terms of reference were therefore quite far-reaching, and its report was presented to Parliament in July 1993. It recommended establishing an independent body to consider suspected miscarriages of justice, where appropriate to arrange for their investigation, and where that investigation revealed matters which should be considered further by the courts, to refer the case to the Court of Appeal. The CCRC is thus a 'last resort', and as such cases cannot be considered until the prisoner has exhausted the normal appeal processes.

---

[14] During the time that this book was being prepared for publication it was intimated to Alex that publishing his story might 'bring the system into disrepute', a basis for his being redetained. Parts of the manuscript were obtained from his probation officer who, quite unwittingly, passed these to the Prison Department without realising that this—and the request to see them— might infringe Alex's legal and human rights.

[15] K Baker (1993), *The Turbulent Years: My Life in Politics*, London: Faber and Faber, pp. 431-432

The CCRC was established in January 1997, and began handling casework from 31 March 1997. It is based in Birmingham, and is accountable to Parliament through the Home Secretary. It has 14 members appointed by the Queen on the recommendation of the Prime Minister, one of whom is designated as chairman—currently Sir Frederick Crawford. The CCRC employs over 60 staff, whose main job is to process and investigate the applications it receives. As of 31 March 1998 the CCRC had received a total of 1,380 applications, including some 280 cases transferred to the CCRC from the Home Office. The CCRC prioritises the cases it receives on the basis of a variety of factors. For example, by date of receipt, and whether or not the applicant is in custody. Other factors are also considered, such as the state of health of the applicant, or important witnesses in the case; the age of the applicant; the possibility of evidence deteriorating or being lost; and, finally, the potential of the case's impact on the criminal justice system.

The CCRC examines each case impartially, and has to decide whether there is a real possibility of it succeeding if it is given a further hearing in an appeal court. However, despite what Baker seems to have intended the CCRC has no powers of investigation, and cannot, for example, carry out searches of premises, check criminal records, use police computers, or make an arrest. Rather it appoints investigating officers from other public bodies such as the DTI, Benefits Agency, Customs and Excise or the police. This might prove problematic, given that the CCRC might have to ask a police force to investigate allegations against members of that force. It should also be remembered that the basis for overturning a conviction is that there are exceptional circumstances—such as a change in the law, or that evidence comes to light that was not available at the time of the trial. This is of relevance to Alex's case, but others still in custody might legitimately question the speed with which the CCRC is able to do this job given the number of cases it has outstanding, and the rate at which it receives new ones.

In Alex's case there would seem to be a basis for appeal on at least two fronts. Firstly the growing evidence to support the theory that he was in fact mistakenly considered a danger to the state, as a consequence of his visit to the Russian Embassy, and the photograph that exists of his talking with Igor Laptev just days before Laptev's deportation on spying charges. Indeed Bill Jarvis was later to confirm that he had seen a hand-written note on Alex's Home Office file confirming that this was the case. This file is not in the public domain. Jarvis himself has gone further than this 'off the record', based on his conversations with some very senior politicians, and would seem to be a valuable witness on Alex's behalf who should be interviewed as soon as possible by any CCRC appointed investigating officer given Mr Jarvis's age. Not only that, this must surely constitute 'new evidence' which was not available at the time—as far as anyone is aware. Whilst this evidence does not go to the heart of the question of Alex's guilt or innocence, it is surely related to this question as it adds credibility to Alex's claims of what happened to him during the original police interviews. It also perhaps explains the police's eagerness, as Alex alleges, to 'fit him up'.

However by far Alex's strongest grounds for appeal relate to the fact that he—for whatever reason—chose to plead guilty, and as a consequence did not put forward any defence at the trial. This confession has to be put into context. As the case of Stefan Kiszko illustrates, the history of British criminal justice is littered with the false confessions of defendants who through undue or illegal pressure exerted on them by investigating officers, or their own psychological make-up or personal circumstances, accept conviction for an offence which they did not commit. Questioned in circumstances that would now be illegal, Alex confessed to a crime despite the fact that he looked nothing like the description of the assailant provided by the principal witness, because he feared that to do otherwise would lead to problems for his family. The evidence that was presented to the court to 'prove' his guilt is less than substantial, and was, Alex claims, largely precipitated by policemen that he feared because of a previous burglary he had committed in Preston. He was young, impressionable, institutionalised, and very much alone. He was also innocent.

These two sets of circumstances thereafter conspired to keep him in custody for twice the length of time that the average murderer receives. Unable to 'acknowledge' his guilt, he is seen as continuing to present a risk to the public—a Catch 22 situation if ever there was one. After all, Mr Justice Cantley, the trial judge recommended that Alex should be released when psychiatric reports considered him fit to be released. Yet positive psychiatric reports from the early 1980s were consistently ignored. Furthermore it would seem safe to conclude that even if he had in fact admitted that he did actually after all commit the offences, he would still have been seen as being a potential threat to the state as a result of his visit to the Russian Embassy all those years previously. Who now has access to the files on Alex containing the secret recommendation that he serve a minimum of 30 years? In short he'd have been damned if he did, and was damned when he did not. There is of course no way of recovering all the years that Alex has lost. Nor is it possible to conclusively 'prove' the theory of a spy conspiracy. What *is* possible is to fight to overturn his conviction, and that is now a matter for the CCRC. They alone have the ability to end this Kafkaesque nightmare, and bring some normality back to Alex's life.

Miscarriages in Alex's case

As a summary I set out below those aspects which contain the potential for demonstrating miscarriage in Alex's case. They are based on Alex's own recollections and claims about how he was treated by the criminal justice system at various stages, my personal knowledge of him as an individual (including searching questions I and others have put to him about the events under consideration), discussions with a range of people who have known Alex over the years and such other relevant information, official or otherwise, as it has been possible to obtain by way of confirmation or corroboration. These aspects should form the basis of an inquiry into his case. Naturally, some of Alex's claims will, legally speaking, only attain full validity when ruled upon by a court or other competent tribunal and to this end some of them will require further investigation, whilst others are self-evident based on information which is already in the public domain:

- Alex was arrested whilst sleeping rough in an office, after breaking in for shelter. About 18 months earlier he had broken into the homes of two police officers in the area. Alex had been told by one of these officers that if he was ever seen in the Preston area again his feet 'wouldn't touch the ground'. These police officers had significant rank—one was an assistant chief constable, and the other an inspector. The police inspector whose home had been broken into became one of the investigating officers in Alex's case.

- All of this lends credence to the fact that when more serious offences happened the police saw these as 'suitable crimes' with which to charge Alex. Aggravated burglary and causing grievous bodily harm were serious enough, and Alex received a discretionary life sentence for these offences, all arising out of the following events: someone broke into the Masterson house carrying a knife. When disturbed that person stabbed Mrs Masterson and then hit her daughter over the head. The assailant then fled. Mrs Masterson was taken to hospital, but released after a few hours. Unfortunately for Alex these events occurred close to the office where he had decided to break in.

- After his arrest Alex was questioned in circumstances which would now be disallowed. He had little sleep, and was kept awake for 48 hours. This involved intense questioning, and a lack of food. Even as the law then stood, these actions should have made the statement prepared by the police, which Alex then signed, inadmissible.

- Witnesses described the assailant as around 30 years old, with black, curly hair. Alex was 18, and had lighter hair. He was refused an identity parade.

- No witnesses were called at the Crown Court because Alex pleaded 'guilty'. No-one therefore had an opportunity to say that the police had got the wrong man. The Mastersons have since been discouraged from talking about the case. The only other evidence, apart from the witness statements, and the statements purportedly made by Alex was: clothing said to be Alex's, but in fact supplied by the police. This never became an official exhibit because Alex pleaded guilty; Alex's notebook, into which, Alex claims, the police entered additional items; a sheath knife which Alex was shown when he was interviewed by the police. He was made to handle it, and through the statement that the police prepared, accept it as part of the evidence against him.

- There is of course Alex's statement, which he has steadfastly maintained was drafted by the investigating officers and as to which there is now corroborative expert evidence to the effect that it could not have been made by Alex on his own account. (Similarly expert evidence points to collusion in the preparation of the police officers' statements, something which, although common practice in the past, is now regarded as wholly unacceptable and as tainting that evidence. Both these are matters for consideration by the CCRC and, hopefully, the Court of Appeal in due course). The 'deal' was that if Alex played along with what was being done then everything would work out fine, and he would get a short sentence. He was also denied access to a lawyer until he appeared in court (or to his parents), and was later discouraged from appealing against his sentence. All the time he was given to believe that if he was compliant he would soon be released. Instead he was pressured and confused from the time of his arrest.

- Alex had been in one kind of institution or another from the age of 12. He could barely read or write, and was fairly inarticulate at that time. He was immature, and his background made him compliant, deferential, and open to suggestion. He was used to doing as he was told by people in authority. Significantly he was accustomed to accepting guilt, and asking for offences to be taken into consideration, whether or not he had committed those offences, so that the police could 'clear them up'.

- Some time previously Alex had visited the Soviet Embassy in London in an effort to trace his Ukrainian grandparents. There he met, and was secretly photographed with Igor Laptev. Later that year Laptev was one of over 100 Russians to be deported. Alex's father was Russian, and they lived in Nelson in Lancashire which was known as 'little Moscow', due to the large numbers of Russian émigrés who lived there.

- Implicit in the circumstances surrounding Alex's 'confession' was a suggestion—generated, Alex claims, by the police—that Alex's father would be thrown out of Britain unless Alex co-operated. Following Alex's arrest two plainclothes policemen visited Alex in his cell, and showed him the photograph that had been taken of him with Igor Laptev. It was put to Alex that he should go inside for a couple of years, which would mean pleading guilty to something which he hadn't done, until the 'heat died down'. If he helped them, they would help Alex's father, and with that Alex colluded in his own 'fit-up'.

- Alex was denied a solicitor until just before his appearance in court, and even his parents were not informed.

- Whilst the offences concerned were serious enough for a custodial sentence, they hardly deserved the one which was passed. Did the public need to be protected from Alex? Nothing in Alex's later medical history suggested that he was a risk, which adds confusion to Mr Justice Cantley's statement at the trial that life sentences were not as bad as they might appear, and that he would be released when doctors were confident that he was safe to be released.

- As a Category A prisoner, and aged just 18 Alex found himself in Britain's toughest prisons, including HMPs Wakefield, Parkhurst, and Gartree—all dispersal prisons. He was never a 'model prisoner' in the early years of his sentence, but then again how would anyone react to being wrongly convicted and then gang-raped? Later in his sentence he absconded from an open prison, refusing to accept his guilt. During this time he wrote letters protesting his innocence to national newspapers, but did not commit further offences.

• Some time earlier, a Birmingham magistrate, Bill Jarvis took up Alex's case, visited the Home Office, and noted that on Alex's file there was a statement 'Not to be released for 30 years'. Inside the file is the photograph of Alex with Igor Laptev. This magistrate has gone further 'off the record' based on his conversations about Alex with some senior Labour politicians.

MK – OK?

Alex was released from HMP Littlehey on 4 July 1993. He had been imprisoned continuously for approaching a quarter of a century, but was allowed only two weeks to prepare himself for a life beyond the prison's walls. Unsurprisingly he was almost totally incapable of settling into his new life in Milton Keynes, and had it not been for the support of friends would undoubtedly have struggled to keep body and soul together, so overwhelmed was he by freedom. His probation officer has found him a one-bedroom flat, which is dominated by the television set that Eric bought for him. The flat itself is strewn with his possessions, newspapers, and personal files, and on entering his room for the first time I was struck by how similar it looked to his cell in HMP Grendon. Perhaps this is deliberate on Alex's part, almost as if he has re-created a sense of prison in his freedom, for he does not see himself as truly free.

Over one roll-up after another, and in between coughs, Alex will explain his circumstances to those who are prepared to listen to him, in the hope that they might be able to provide some help in ensuring him justice. Meanwhile he has successfully applied for Disability Living Allowance, and is very frail. He struggles to walk for more than a few minutes, and unsurprisingly has never been able to find work. He is consumed by a deep sense of injustice that constantly gnaws away at him, and he has almost put his life on hold until matters have been made right.

Alex, in a memorable phrase from *Prison Chronicles*, is still an 'underwater swimmer', only this time he is trying to catch his breath with the CCRC, a life licence, and the Probation Service. Who knows what the future will bring for Alex, but is it really too much to hope that British justice—'the best in the World'—might at long last bring the longest injustice to an end?

The last word
It is only right that the last word in the book should go to Alex. Having decided to participate once more with the project, he wrote to me not only summarising his own section, but also saying that he saw his miscarraige in a wider context.

> I have no doubt that the Home Office knew all along that I was innocent. There is evidence today which points that way. Why then seek to keep someone locked away for something they hadn't done? Was it to save the system embarrassment? For whatever reason, a gross miscarriage of justice was done and allowed to continue. I was lucky, I had people campaigning for me and sending me letters of support. There are people still held in captivity in this country who are suffering wrongful imprisonment but who have no-one to campaign for them or keep their spirits raised. They exist, and while they do the concept of British justice is undermined and stands indicted of corruption.

A Guide to Further Reading

There is a wealth of research and published material available about crime and punishment, and this section is therefor only intended as a broad guide. For a general introduction to the work of HM Prison Service see Nick Flynn's *Introduction to Prisons and Imprisonment*. This is the most current introductory book available about prisons, written by the deputy director of the Prison Reform Trust (PRT), and is very accessible to the general reader. Also of considerable use for people wanting greater detail is Mark Leech's *The Prisons Handbook*, which also lists all of the prisons in Britain, their telephone numbers, addresses, key personnel, and extracts from the most recent HM Chief Inspector of Prison's reports about each individual prison. *The Prison Governors: Theory and Practice* by Shane Bryans and David Wilson explains the crucial role of prison governors and outlines the importance of prison cultures.

There is a growing interest in the work of HMP Grendon, although this is still rather confined to specialist journals. However of interest to the general reader is *Grendon: A Study of a Therapeutic Prison* by Elaine Genders and Elaine Player, Frank Cook's *Hard Cell* and Mark Leech's *A Product of the System*. (The latter two books written by former inmates at Grendon). There has been comparatively little interest in life sentenced prisoners. An exceptions are *Murderers and Life Imprisonment* by Eric Cullen and Tim Newell and Clare Sparks' *Prisoners' Views of the Lifer System*.

The most accessible and academic book with regard to the law and its impact on prisons remains *Prison Law: Text and Materials* by Stephen Livingstone and Tim Owen. A variety of popular books remain in print about famous miscarriages of justice. Of special interest are Paul Foot's *Murder at the Farm: Who Killed Carl Bridgewater*, *Innocents: How Justice Failed Stefan Kiszko and Lesley Molseed* by Jonathan Rose, Steve Panter and Trevor Wilkinson and *Anybody's Nightmare: The Sheila Bowler Story* by Angela and Tim Devlin. For readers who want to put all of this into the context of the criminal justice system as a whole, see *What Everyone in Britain Should Know About Crime and Punishment*, by David Wilson and John Ashton (1998).

Bibliographical details of these and other publications mentioned in the text are as follows:

K Baker (1993), *The Turbulent Years: My Life in Politics*, London: Faber and Faber

J Boyle (1977), *A Sense of Freedom*, London: Pan Books

S Bryans, D Wilson (1998), *The Prison Governor: Theory and Practice*, Leyhill: Prison Service Journal

F Cook (1998), *Hard Cell*, Liverpool: Blue Coat Press

E Cullen, T Newell (1999), *Murderers and Life Imprisonment: Containment, Treatment, Safety and Risk*, Winchester: Waterside Press

A Devlin, T Devlin (1998), *Anybody's Nightmare: The Sheila Bowler Story*, Staplehurst, Taverner

N Flynn (1998), *Introduction to Prisons and Imprisonment*, Winchester: Waterside Press

P Foot (1986), *Murder at the Farm: Who Killed Carl Bridgewater?*, Harmondsworth: Penguin

E Genders, E Player (1995), *Grendon: A Study of a Therapeutic Community*, Oxford: Clarendon Press

W J Gray (1973), 'The English Prison Medical Service', in G Wolstenholme, M O'Connor (Eds.), *The Medical Care of Prisoners and Detainees*, Amsterdam: Elsevier

M Leech (1992), *A Product of the System*, London: Victor Gollancz

M Leech (1998), *The Prisons Handbook*, Winchester: Waterside Press

Lifer Manual: A Guide for Members of the Prison and Probation Services Working With Life Sentenced Prisoners (1996), HM Prison Service

S Livingstone, T Owen (1993), *Prison Law: Text and Materials,* Oxford: Clarendon Press
P Marshall (1997), *A Re-conviction Study of HMP Grendon Therapeutic Community,* Home Office Research and Statistics Directorate, Research Findings No. 53
D Rose (1996), *In the Name of the Law: The Collapse of Criminal Justice,* London: Vintage
J Rose, S Panter, T Wilkinson (1997), *Innocents: How Justice Failed Stefan Kiszko and Lesley Moleseed,* London: Fourth Estate
R Sapsford (1983), 'Indeterminacy: Memorandum to the House of Lords Committee on Murder and Life Imprisonment'
R Sapsford (1993), *Life Sentenced Prisoners: Reaction, Response and Change,* Milton Keynes: Open University Press
Sparks, C (1999), *Prisoners' Views of the Lifer System,* London: Prison Reform Trust
D Wilson, J Ashton (1998), *What Everyone in Britain Should Know About Crime and Punishment,* London: Blackstone Press
Lord Justice Woolf (1991), *Prison Disturbances, April 1990 - Report of an Inquiry,* Cm 1456, London: HMSO

Cases Cited in the Text

Becker v Home Office [1972] 2 QB 407
Golder v United Kingdom (1975) 1 EHRR 524, Series A, No. 18
R v Board of Visitors of Hull Prison, ex parte St Germain [1979] QB 425
Raymond v Honey [1983] 1 AC 1
Thynne, Wilson and Gunnell v United Kingdom (1990), 13 EHRR 666, Series A, No. 190
Weeks v United Kingdom (1987), 10 EHRR 1, Series A, No. 26

Index

The WATERSIDE PRESS Prison List - *Opening up a closed world*

The Prisons Handbook Mark Leech
'A tour de force through current penal policy and practice' *Prison Service Journal*
'A must for anyone involved with prisoners or imprisonment' *New Law Journal*
THIRD EDITION 1999. ISBN 1 872 870 72 4. £37.50 plus £3.50 p&p

Murderers and Life Imprisonment: Containment, Treatment, Safety and Risk Eric Cullen and Tim Newell. Foreword by Stephen Shaw, Director, Prison Reform Trust. 1999 ISBN 1872 870 56 2. £18 plus £2 p&p

Prison Patter Angela Devlin A dictionary of prison slang. 'Useful for the custody suite' *Police Journal*. 1996 ISBN 1 872 870 41 4. £12 plus £2 p&p

Invisible Women: What's Wrong With Women's Prisons Angela Devlin. 'What an excellent book!' *Justice of the Peace*. 1998 ISBN 1 872 870 59 7. £18 plus £2 p&p

Punishments of Former Days Ernest Pettifer 'A good read' *The Magistrate*. 1992 ISBN 1 872 870 05 8. £12 plus £2 p&p

Introduction to Prisons and Imprisonment Nick Flynn. Foreword by Lord Hurd of Westwell. 'A comprehensive and clear overview' *The Magistrate*. 1998 ISBN 1 872 870 37 6. £13.50 plus £2 p&p

Prisons of Promise Tessa West. Foreword by Sir David Ramsbotham, Chief Inspector of Prisons. 'Extremely well-researched' *Justice of the Peace*. 1997 ISBN 1 872 870 50 3. £16 plus £2 p&p

Deaths of Offenders: The Hidden Side of Justice Alison Liebling (Ed.) Examines deaths in police, prison and special hospital custody—including in court and police cells. 1998 ISBN 1 872 870 61 9. £16 plus £2 p&p

Criminal Classes: Offenders at School Angela Devlin 'If you are in any doubt about the links between poor education, crime and recidivism, read it': Marcel Berlins *The Guardian*. 1995 ISBN 1 872 870 30 9. £16 plus £2 p&p

I'm Still Standing Bob Turney The autobiography of a dyslexic ex-prisoner, now a probation officer. 'A truly remarkable book' *Prison Writing*. 1997 ISBN 1 872 870 43 0. £13.50 plus £2 p&p

The Longest Injustice Alex Alexandrowicz and David Wilson. Alex spent 22 years in custody protesting his innocence. This book seeks to discover how something which began with him wrongly pleading guilty in the belief that he would get a 'short' sentence turned into a Kafkaesque nightmare. Alex's story is placed in perspective by Professor David Wilson. ISBN 1 872 870 45 7. £16 plus £2 p&p

WATERSIDE PRESS • WINCHESTER • 01962 855567
VISA/MASTERCARD
E-mail:watersidepress@compuserve.com
Bookshop:http//www.penlex.org.uk